# The SeX Addiction

## PROVEN STRATEGIES TO HELP YOU REGAIN CONTROL OF YOUR LIFE

TAMARA PENIX SBRAGA, PH.D.
WILLIAM T. O'DONOHUE, PH.D.
Foreword by JOHN BANCROFT, MD

New Harbinger Publications, Inc.

Distributed in Canada by Raincoast Books

Copyright © 2003 by Tamara Penix Sbraga and William T. O'Donohue
New Harbinger Publications, Inc.
5674 Shattuck Avenue
Oakland, CA 94609

Cover design by Amy Shoup
Edited by Kayla Sussell
Text design by Tracy Marie Carlson

ISBN 1-57224-376-7 Paperback

New Harbinger Publications' Web site address: www.newharbinger.com

08      07      06

10    9    8    7    6    5    4    3

*To Connie and Michael Thompson, Jason, Linda and Logan Penix, Nathan Penix and Marti Fuentes, and especially Pierluigi Sbraga. Thank you for your steadfast love and encouragement.*

—Tamara Penix Sbraga

*To my family, teachers, and students for all the support, lessons, and encouragement they have given me.*

—Bill O'Donohue

# Contents

## Part One
### Nothing I Do Turns Out the Way It's Supposed To

## Part Four
Mastering Your Domain

## Part Five
Life Is Beautiful

# Acknowledgments

We would like to acknowledge the dissertation committee that assisted in the development of the book and the first study of its effectiveness in changing sexual behavior. Thank you Victoria Follette, D. Richard Laws, and Mark Waldo. We would also like to thank the clients and research participants who trusted us with information about their sexual self-control problems and who worked valiantly to change them. We expect your forthrightness to change many lives beyond your own. We also owe many thanks to the clinicians and researchers who contributed to the relapse prevention and cognitive behavioral therapy literature we've integrated to create this treatment program. We humbly stand on the shoulders of giants. Lastly, we would like to acknowledge the contributions of our editors, Tesilya Hanauer and Kayla Sussell. Thank you for your dedication to bringing this book to those who need it.

# Foreword

Being out of control in our sexual lives can lead to major problems. An inability to refrain from spending hours on the Internet for sexual pleasure, from spending money on explicit sexual material, from pursuing new and typically casual sexual encounters, for example, can cause havoc in our primary relationships, our work roles, and our personal well-being. Although we have no good data on the prevalence of such problems, they appear to be escalating at an alarming rate, possibly because of the impact of modern technology, in particular the Internet, in providing ever-increasing access to an endless array of sexual stimuli or interactions.

The terms "sexual addiction" and "sexual compulsivity" are currently fashionable, although the extent to which out-of-control sexual behavior can be understood as a form of addiction or as an example of compulsivity, as usually defined, is not yet clear. There is much we don't understand. In particular, we do not understand why some people get into this "out-of-control" state, whereas most of us don't. Is this the result of our genes, or early learning, or difficulties dealing with intimacy?

Recent research at the Kinsey Institute has been looking at two aspects of sexuality which vary considerably from person to person, and which may eventually help us to understand out-of-control sexual behavior better. One involves the tendency to inhibit or "switch off" sexual arousal when in a situation that is risky or likely to lead to problems. The need for this adaptive inhibition is clearly evident in other animals as well as humans: sex is something that can get animals into trouble, as well as humans.

But humans appear to vary considerably in the tendency to inhibit sexuality in this way. For most of us, there is enough inhibition to make it possible to manage our sexual lives sensibly. Some of us inhibit too much, and are vulnerable to sexual dysfunctions as a result. And then there are those who are low in such inhibitory patterns. They, we have found, are more likely to take sexual risks, and further research may show that "low inhibition" of this kind increases the likelihood of developing sexual addictions.

The second factor concerns the impact of negative mood on our sexuality. Most people, when they are feeling depressed or anxious, find their interest in sex and their capacity for sexual response goes down. But, again, we find an interesting minority where the reverse applies. We have already shown this pattern to be present in many "sex addicts," as well as being linked to high-risk sexual behavior. The sexual behavior can be seen as a short-term way of feeling better, even though this is quickly followed by an emotional worsening as the person realizes "it's happened again." As we progress with such research we probably will find a range of contributory factors, which will vary in importance from case to case.

But one thing is already fairly clear. Whatever the cause, once out-of-control sexual behavior starts to affect us, then we have to take personal responsibility for getting our sexual lives back under control. There is not going to be an easy solution or a magic pill. It is essential that each person affected in this way gains some understanding of the important factors in his or her case. If, for example, it becomes clear to you that you are more likely to get out-of-control sexually when you are depressed or anxious, then you need to learn to recognize the pattern at an early stage in the sequence, so that you can practice and use other ways to improve your mood that will have less destructive consequences.

The *Sex Addiction Workbook*, by Drs. Tamara Penix Sbraga and William O'Donohue, is an excellent starting point for learning how to grapple with such problems. It will help you to recognize the wide range of coping strategies that are possible and to focus on the ones most likely to help in your case. Establishing your priorities for the use of your time, and recognizing, by careful monitoring of your behavior, the key links in your typical behavioral sequence, are important aspects of the process. This book is well designed to mobilize and sustain your own motivation to change, and to provide practical steps and programs that will enable you to implement that change. Keep it close by you as you work to regain control of your sexual life and to reestablish the real benefits that a controlled and responsible sex life can bring to you.

—John Bancroft, MD
Director, Kinsey Institute
Bloomington, IN

# Preface

This book is unique in treating out-of-control sexual behaviors because it is the first of its kind to have been created with what really works in mind. This book is based on strategies that have been proven to change sexual behaviors.

Research has shown that the techniques presented on the following pages help change thoughts, feelings, and behaviors. In addition, an earlier version of this book was tested to see if it could help change people's out-of-control sexual behaviors. It worked. Fifty-four research participants using the book and reporting on their use of it said the following after using the book: They knew more about how to control their sexual behavior than they did when they started. Their sexual problems decreased in frequency and severity. They also found the book useful, interesting, and believable. A second study of the book is in progress using a larger group of people with even more severe problems controlling their sexuality. We are committed to bringing you the most useful and effective information about changing your sexual behavior, and we wish you all the best in making the changes you want to make.

# Introduction

This is the book for you if

- You're worried that your secret sex life might be discovered.

- You're embarrassed by your sexual desires and activities.

- Some of your sexual actions make you feel guilty.

- You feel silly or crazy because you're constantly risking your marriage, job, or good name for sex.

- You feel dirty or immoral.

- You know you are a sex addict.

- You feel your sexual activities are "out of control."

- Your sexual actions trample your basic rules and beliefs.

- You waste your time and money on things like porn magazines, prostitutes, X-rated pay-per-view porn, or the Internet.

- You have a sexual disorder such as pedophilia, exhibitionism, or voyeurism.

- You're hurting someone you love by being dishonest or unfaithful.

- Your sex life puts you at high risk for contracting a sexually transmitted disease or dying from AIDS.

- Sex is always disconnected from love, caring, or being close to the person with whom you have sex.

- You are never satisfied sexually.

- You become tired of your sex partners as soon as you have sex with them.

- You'd like to quit cruising places to pick up someone, following people you find attractive, lying, covering up, or making excuses to yourself and others.

- When you hear about people in sexual trouble, you think it could easily be you.

- You think some of the things you have done sexually are illegal or have hurt other people.

- You make promises to yourself about controlling your sex life, and you always break those promises.

- You keep to yourself so that others won't suspect what you do in your free time.

- You make complicated plans about what would really satisfy you sexually.

- You can't afford what you're spending on your sex habits.

- You can't concentrate on what you need to do because thoughts about sex often take over your mind.

- You are constantly searching for the perfect sexual experience.

## Who This Book Is For

This book is for everyone who thinks they might have a problem controlling what they do sexually. It covers many separate sexual problems, but these problems share important commonalties. Not every example will apply directly to every person who reads this book, but most will apply at least indirectly to your problem and will help you find some solutions. This goal of this book is to help you figure out ways to control your sexual behavior so you can stop looking over your shoulder and start having a satisfying life.

If you find yourself reading some of the real-life stories that follow and you say, "You know, my problem isn't so bad, maybe I don't need this," you're probably at least partly wrong. In our therapy work with people who have sexual self-control problems, we've found that no matter what the problem is, whether it's calling phone-sex numbers or pushing other people to have sex, the causes of these behaviors and the treatment are basically the same.

You've probably tried to change on your own and haven't succeeded for very long. That's not surprising and it doesn't mean you're a failure. The fact that you've tried to control the problem is impressive. Changing sexual practices is not easy. In fact, because of the ways our bodies work, sexual habits may be one of the most difficult sets of habits to change. The pleasure produced by sexual activity makes us want to have more of it. Still, if you've picked up this book, it's clear that you're motivated to begin to do battle with your strong sexual urges. We can help turn your determination into results with scientifically supported solutions. Give this book a chance and give yourself the opportunity to create a pleasurable sex life that doesn't hold you hostage to shame, guilt, fear, remorse, and all those other unpleasant feelings that result from out-of-control sexual behavior. If you try the strategies that follow, there is a good chance that your life will change for the better. You'll never know until you try.

> *No matter what the sexual problem is, the causes and treatment are the same.*

## A Public Epidemic

What do Bill Clinton, Hugh Grant, Wilt Chamberlain, Pee Wee Herman, a young, married teacher in Minnesota, Mexican pop star Gloria Trevi, pop idol Michael Jackson, a senior class president, a lumber delivery man, an executive at Disney, the former head of the Roman Catholic Church in Austria, several Japanese businessmen, and many tourists to Tobago, Kenya, Cambodia, Thailand, Cuba, Indonesia, Russia, Vietnam, and the Philippines have in common? They have all been publicly implicated and embarrassed for lapses of sexual self-control. This list just scratches the surface of the millions of people who are getting into sexual trouble. Their sexual practices are ruining their lives. They face embarrassment, loss of jobs, family, good health, money, and reputation, even criminal prosecution. Do you want to avoid adding your name to this roster?

## CBT: A Scientifically Proven Method for Sexual Self-Control

This book will introduce you to the most advanced scientific methods for making the most out of your sex life and getting a handle on those parts of it that are out of control. The techniques are based on a revolutionary form of treatment called *cognitive behavioral therapy* (CBT). This is the first form of therapy that has compiled a great deal of scientific evidence proving that it works to help some people change the way they operate. "Cognition" is another word for mental processes, or thoughts. So, CBT is a treatment that works on thoughts and behavior, or actions. Nothing could be more suited to the problems of sexual self-control. Thoughts and fantasies often get the problem started, and your later behavior regularly leaves you feeling ashamed, guilty, and unsatisfied. Cognitive behavioral therapy attacks both parts of the problem.

Some people are skeptical about quick treatments and self-help approaches. They think treatment must be done over a long time in a room with a doctor for it to work. But many of the most effective treatments for problems ranging from mild anxiety to major depression are cognitive-behavioral and short term. Many involve the reader with the same type of personal practices you will be doing with this book.

*Cognitive behavioral therapy is effective.*

There is not a lot of evidence that long-term psychotherapy helps people to learn to control their sexual desires. Many of you may have tried it, without seeing any results. However, in many places all over America, Canada, Europe, and New Zealand, research has shown that cognitive-behavioral treatments have helped some people to control themselves sexually (Beckett et al. 1994; Hudson et al. 1995; Marques et al. 2000; Marshall and Anderson, 1996).

## Cognitive Behavioral Techniques for Sexual Self-Control

Some techniques for sexual self-control have proved to be surprisingly effective for some people and some sexual problems. There are studies that suggest, for problems of sexual self-control, cognitive behavior therapy may be superior to any other type of therapy, including psychodynamic psychotherapy, psychoanalysis, and client-centered therapy (Hall 1995). Because many mental health professionals are interested in what really works to change problematic sexual behavior, these hopeful findings have initiated many scientific investigations into effective treatments for sexual self-control problems.

A 1999 article by Grossman, Martis, and Fichtner concluded that the majority of the evidence suggests that the cognitive behavioral treatment approaches you are about to learn are effective in significantly reducing the out-of-control sexual actions of some people. *This is the best-studied approach to the treatment of problematic sexual behavior that currently exists.* A study by the authors demonstrated that, for men with problems ranging from excessive use of pornography and phone sex to exhibitionism, there was a significant reduction in the severity and frequency of the losses of sexual self-control (Sbraga and O'Donohue, under review). In clinical studies, cognitive behavioral therapy has been shown to be as effective as drug therapy for controlling some sexual desires and actions, without the occasionally nasty side effects of drug treatment (Grossman, Martis, and Fichtner, 1999).

Although hormone therapies are useful in some severe cases of sexual self-control problems, there is now an effective approach to overcome these problems without the need for these medications. The best part is, you don't have to leave your home to get help. In the past, you would have had to visit a doctor or mental health worker to get help for your problem. Just the idea of revealing personal, possibly embarrassing, or even incriminating information about your sex life probably kept you away, kept you from seeking help, and left you suffering, worried, and alone.

With CBT treatment it may be possible for you to treat your problem by yourself just with this book and the determination to try out the various approaches you will encounter. In this case, determination means more than just thinking about doing something or just having a positive attitude toward change. It means trying out the suggestions, taking risks, and behaving differently.

The information and skills you will learn from this book are not complicated. It's a bit like using a computer for the first time. At first, all of those different keys and functions may seem confusing and intimidating. But, of course, after you study the manual, you figure out what everything does, you practice, and, eventually, you use the computer without thinking. You can develop new and useful habits in the same way.

## Treatment Doesn't Have to Be Complicated to Work

Controlling sexual behavior can be likened to learning how to use a computer. At first, you must learn to pay attention to all of the things that are associated with your sexual behavior, even things that seem unrelated. For example, having Internet access may seem unrelated to loss of sexual self-control. But, if you meet new sex partners (some of them claiming to be underage) in Internet chat rooms, clearly that's not the best place for you to spend your time.

## Why We Wrote This Book

We wrote this book so you can learn about the methods that are helping so many other people to overcome their problems of sexual self-control and improve their self-esteem and their lives. As you try out each new suggestion, you will learn something about yourself, and you will learn how to live your life differently.

Imagine the sense of accomplishment you'll feel when you have mastered these techniques, when controlling your sex life is no longer a problem. Think about what would it be like to have a clear conscience, to be free of the fear of getting busted and able to think about other matters besides sex. You have a chance to rewrite your own history without the big scandal at the end. This is your chance to focus on what is truly important and to make a life you want to live, one that will bring you more peace and greater happiness.

## Dr. O'Donohue

Several paths led to our development of this treatment. Dr. O'Donohue got his first job as a psychologist in Maine. He was curious about problems of sexual self-control and was referred a number of patients who were suffering as a result of the pain they had caused themselves, their victims, their loved ones, and their victims' loved ones because of their inability to control their strong urges to have sex.

He knew that there weren't any well-studied treatments for the problems he was seeing. Throughout his years as a professor at Northern Illinois University, he had been frustrated with the lack of useful information and had decided to focus his career on the study of sexual control. He conducted studies of sexual arousal and on how people talk about their sexual fantasies. He learned how to help patients care about the people who were involved in their sex lives. Over time, Dr. O'Donohue has written and edited more than a hundred articles and books, many of them about sexual self-control. Nevertheless, in spite of all this new information, there is still much more to learn about sexual self-control. While the research continues, there are those who need help today who can benefit from what has been discovered so far. Dr. O'Donohue is committed to getting useful information out to the people who need it.

## Dr. Penix Sbraga

Dr. Penix Sbraga's interest in sex addiction began with her interest in child sexual abuse. After getting two degrees in psychology, she took some time to discover the area of psychology in which she wanted to specialize. As she read about abused children, she realized not very much had been written about the people doing the harm. Her investigations into sexual self-control began by going to the source.

She began working as a psychologist with sex offenders and others in a state penitentiary. There, she treated people incarcerated for sex crimes and encountered many others suffering from sexual self-control problems, such as exhibitionism, voyeurism, trying to push unwilling partners into sex, obsessive use of pornography, and more. Dr. Penix Sbraga began her research by studying everything that had been written about sexuality and sexual control. She discovered that there were effective treatments for improving sexual self-control in some individuals, but they weren't being widely used, mainly because clinicians didn't know much about them. Therapists are often too busy to keep up with advancements in treatment. There are no universally accepted standards dictating the practices of those who treat sexual self-control problems.

In 1997, Dr. Penix Sbraga received a research grant from the National Institutes of Health to develop a computer program to teach counselors the latest techniques in changing problematic sexual behaviors. Soon afterward she realized that most people would never have the chance to receive that kind of treatment since it's mainly offered to those who've already gotten into trouble because of their sexual conduct. It was obvious to her that most people would never want to visit someone for help with sex addictions. Asking for help for a sexual self-control problem may feel humiliating, and many people also have doubts about whether they can be helped. Who would want to spend money to talk about their sex lives and not be able to be helped?

## A Reasonable Solution

Drs. Penix Sbraga and O'Donohue have brought together the best known techniques for controlling sexual behavior in this book. Not every story and approach will apply to you or your problem. But, chances are good that most of them will apply in some way, and if you try working with some of them, your behavior and your life will change dramatically.

No one else has to know you are using this book. It's not the type of reading material that airline passengers read during flights. Read it in private. Mark it up. Tear out pages if you want to put them in your wallet as reminders. This book is a tool, as useful as any you are likely to find. Use it like one. Don't cut corners, don't ignore details, and don't save the hard parts for later. You've got to use this book as if you mean it.

*If you try, change will happen.*

### Case Example: John

John was a college student who also worked for a mail service. He called for help because he was becoming suicidal. He had a girlfriend and hardworking parents who were becoming increasingly concerned about him as he became more and more depressed. He was spending hundreds of dollars a week on pornography and prostitutes and he couldn't seem to stop. His ability to concentrate was gone and he was failing courses at school. All he could think about was sex. He also knew that, eventually, someone would find out about his sexual habits. He was disgusted with himself, and was just waiting for his life to fall apart. John was skeptical that anyone would be able to help him. He thought he was a "worthless cause."

Since he had nothing to lose, John decided to follow some of the suggestions you will find in this book. In a matter of weeks he started to feel better and began to get his life under control. He started to get a handle on the thoughts and emotions that seemed to drive his every move. He figured out ways to change his surroundings so he would be less focused on sex. For example, he got rid of his satellite television and Internet access. He made himself temporarily accountable to his parents for his bank account balance. He discovered the secrets of better controlling his high sex drive and began to have a more satisfying sex life. He created a balanced life. John is just one of the many thousands of clients who have benefited from the techniques presented in this book.

You don't have to be at the end of your rope to get help for your problem. You don't have to wait until your life comes crumbling down around you, although many people do. Anyone can benefit from the information and strategies we discuss within this book. From time to time, almost everyone has to deal with strong sexual temptations and sometimes it's hard to know what to do so as not to ruin the life you really want.

This book will show you exactly what to do when temptation arises. The training is clear and straightforward. You will receive the practical help you need to get some relief and to make a better life for yourself. The approach really works and you'll be surprised by how much better your life can be. One of the most frequent comments we hear in therapy is, "I wish I'd done this sooner." Don't put it off. Don't let your misery grow and don't lose time you'll never recapture. Turn to chapter 1, and start changing your life today.

# Part One

# Nothing I Do Turns Out the Way It's Supposed To

# Chapter One

# What's the Problem?

## The Myth of Sexual Self-Control

For some strange reason people are always surprised when acquaintances or famous people they admire get into sexual trouble. People are shocked and amazed when a beloved priest is accused of molesting kids in his Sunday school class, an elementary school teacher confesses her pregnancy by a twelve-year-old student, the host of a children's television show is found masturbating in a porn theater, or the president of the United States faces impeachment for receiving oral sex from an intern. It's headline news. People talk endlessly about the scandal, how their beliefs about a person have been shattered, and how they never thought that the person they knew, or a person with such outstanding qualities, could do such a thing.

You probably know better than anyone that most people are wrong in their basic beliefs about how sex fits with other aspects of life. People generally assume that you can't be a good priest, teacher, children's television host, or the president and have sexual self-control problems. They think that if someone is good at these jobs, that person must be a master of self-control. That's exactly where many people make a serious mistake. Many different kinds of people are good at keeping sexual secrets. As you know very well, people can accomplish a lot in the other areas of their lives and still have a real problem, even a dangerous problem, with sex.

## Basic Assumptions about Sex Can Be Wrong

Even you may have fallen into this thinking trap. It's entirely possible that, like so many others, you've said to yourself that you don't really have a problem because you are holding down a job and others don't know anything about your secrets. Or you may say to yourself that you do what you do at certain acceptable levels and, in any case, you are planning to stop soon.

Unfortunately, sex can often be like a mythical monster that's never satisfied with the limits you place on it. The beast requires more and more sacrifices to keep it quiet. Many people put their security at risk, including jobs, money, relationships, and health, to meet the ever-increasing demands of their sex lives. Typically, they can't keep up the pace. They vow to stop because the pressure can become very intense. But the demand is still there. It's like being on a treadmill that keeps speeding up. You feel as though you're just waiting for the day when you'll fall flat on your face in front of everyone.

The good news is that you don't have to wait for that day to come. You can stop the machine and get off right now. You just have to start by being honest with yourself, painfully honest.

# Sexual Addiction Defined

When people talk about sexual addiction problems, often they're referring to the sexual disorders described in the *Diagnostic and Statistical Manual of Mental Disorders IV* (DSM), the definitive reference of the American Psychiatric Association, which is updated every few years (American Psychiatric Association 2000). This is the book all mental health professionals in the United States use as a guide in the diagnosis and treatment of psychological and behavioral problems. The sexual disorders included in the DSM include exhibitionism (exposing yourself), fetishism (seeking sexual satisfaction from one part of a person or an object), frotteurism (obtaining sexual satisfaction by rubbing against a person or object), masochism (wanting to have pain inflicted on you during sex), pedophilia (sexual contact with children), sadism (causing pain to others during sex), voyeurism (watching unsuspecting people undressing or having sex), and other more individualistic problems, such as making obscene phone calls.

On the other hand, when some people consider sexual problems, they think of criminal sexual behavior such as rape. This book addresses the whole range of sexual-control difficulties that cause problems for people and those around them. These include activities that may not be illegal and are not considered disorders, but they still cause trouble. Among these are the following:

- Frequenting prostitutes

- Using pornography obsessively

- Engaging in Internet and telephone sex

- Having serial affairs

- Frequenting massage parlors

- Going to strip clubs obsessively

- Going to bathhouses for sex

- Frequenting topless bars obsessively

- Feeling driven to have sex many times a day

We do not view any sexual behaviors as actual addictions in the way that using heroin is an actual addiction, but we've adopted the terminology because it is the language people use to talk about the loss of sexual self-control. Understand that we are not taking a moralistic stance against all of these behaviors or saying they are out-and-out wrong. That's not the message here. What's important is that, for many people, these behaviors *do* result in significant harm to themselves and others, whether it's through obvious physical and/or mental pain, or less obvious damage caused by the loss of money and productivity, the lack of ability to concentrate, the time spent away from families, work, or meaningful relationships, and the lost opportunities to become involved in life-enriching activities.

## Case Example: Michael Ryan

Michael Ryan, a Princeton professor and award-winning poet from Boston, knows what it means to lose everything to an all-consuming sex life. Sex was not a part of Michael Ryan's life. It *was* his life for more than twenty years. In writing about his life, Ryan reports that he was always on the prowl for sex, particularly when he landed a teaching job at Princeton University. He wrote, "My primary loyalty was to sex. No human relationship took precedence over it. Not marriage, not friendship, and certainly not ethics" (Ryan, 1995 p. 4). He seduced students, flight attendants, his health care providers, and countless others while drifting through two failed marriages. He was fired from the university for his sexual activities with students, but even that hardship didn't faze him. He finally realized the extent of his problem when he planned to have sex with the fifteen-year-old daughter of a friend. Ryan lost relationships, career, reputation, income, health, and self-respect before he finally got treatment.

This wasn't an issue of a professor having a relationship with a younger woman, or another adult for that matter. Such relationships may very well be consensual and enjoyable for the partner. The problem was the uncontrolled nature of the behaviors requiring

- Extensive plotting and planning

- Time, energy, and attention stolen from other productive activities

- The need to up the ante in the numbers of sexual encounters, partners, and novelties in sexual experiences

- The use of other people as objects to be used and discarded when they had served his satisfaction

- The need to move on to bigger and better (more "perfect") sexual highs

When sex dominates one's life over all other interests, that is troubling. The life out of balance is cause for concern. This kind of imbalance leads to major losses for the out-of-control person and those around him or her. Is your life out of balance because of sex? See if you can identify yourself in the following quiz.

## Exercise: Are You Out of Control?

**Directions:** Find a quiet, private place and answer the following questions as candidly as possible. Using a pen or pencil, place a checkmark at the end of each question that is true of you. Be as honest with yourself as you know how to be. At the end of the quiz, add up the number of your checkmarks and you'll be clearer about what your particular sexual problem is like and how it fits into the range of sexual self-control problems. You may feel uncomfortable while you take this test. That's normal. It's like going to the gym for the first time. It's tough at first, but people get through it. As they say at the gym, "No pain, no gain."

1. Do you wake up in the morning and fall asleep at night planning new sexual encounters? _____

2. Do you use the Internet to get or keep yourself sexually stimulated at work or at home? _√_

3. Do you have a secret collection of porn, whether pictures, magazines, videos, or computer images? _____

4. Do you make yourself sexually available to others even if you are in a serious relationship with someone? _____

5. Do you spend money you need for other expenses on sex or sex-related bills? _____

6. Do you spend time cruising for sex partners? _____

7. Do you use sex to make yourself feel better? _√_

8. Do you like to dominate others when you have sex? _____

9. Have you had more sexual partners than you can remember? _____

10. Is your free time consumed by sexual fantasizing, planning, masturbating, or other sexual activities? ✓

11. Do you find yourself in places you would be ashamed to be caught in (such as brothels, bathhouses, strip clubs, sex shows)? _____

12. Do you lie to people you care about in regard to what you are doing sexually? _____

13. Do you keep people at a distance for fear they might find out about your other life? _____

14. Do you look for weak, naive, or vulnerable people for sexual encounters? _____

15. Are your sexual experiences frequently disappointing? ✓

16. Have you almost been caught and vowed to stop what you do sexually, only to start again? _____

17. Do you feel controlled by your sexual drive or sexual desires? ✓

18. Are there certain sexual thoughts you can't get rid of, no matter how you try? _____

19. Are you isolated and lonely? ✓

20. Have you lost a job, relationship, or home due to your sexual activities? _____

**Scoring:** Add up the number of items you checked, and score yourself according to the following scale.

**None**  Congratulations! It looks as if you are doing better than you thought. If you've been really frank with yourself, you can skim through this book to pick up some interesting facts and prevent future sexual difficulties.

**1–2**  There's reason to be concerned that you may have the beginnings of a sexual self-control problem. It may not be full-blown at this point, but the sooner you tackle it, the less likely it will take over your life.

**3–5**  You have a significant sexual self-control problem that affects several parts of your life. From the outside it may look as if your life is in order, but it's just a matter of time before you get into real trouble. Begin applying the methods you'll learn in this book immediately to turn the tide in the other direction.

**6–10**  You have a serious sexual self-control problem that is consuming your life. You can't make it through the day without fantasizing about, planning, and engaging in risky sexual encounters. You're under intense pressure and feel completely controlled by your sexual desires. You need to begin applying the techniques you will find in this book today.

**11–15**   As you probably already know, your sexuality is out of control. You are consumed by sexual fantasies, sexual planning, and sexual activities. You have already faced serious losses because of your sexual behavior and you risk more losses every day. You need to begin investing significant time and attention toward changing your behavior. Start with the methods suggested in this book. Apply them faithfully and examine the results. If you do not see the results you want, and you and others are still being hurt by your actions, enlist more help. Find a therapist who specializes in sexual problems and work on your problems together with the therapist.

**16+**   You have a sexual self-control problem that has reached a dangerous level. Begin to apply the techniques in this book today with the guidance of a therapist who specializes in the treatment of sexual problems. You have probably already faced serious trouble due to your sexual behaviors. Consider that warning carefully. You may be able to avoid more critical losses if you become involved in treatment right now. Don't put it off.

   This quiz was provided to give you a way to measure the seriousness of your problem. Everyone must start somewhere. It's possible that your sexual behavior has been out of control for years. Maybe it's only been months. Whatever the case, it's time to do something about it. If you have a higher score, that may mean you must do more work, but let's face facts. You spent a lot of time getting into this mess. It's going to take some effort to get out of it. Everyone can make it to the finish line, whether they have ten miles or ten thousand to go. The crucial move is to take that first step in the right direction.
   Millions of people are silently struggling with the same sorts of troubles you face every day. They think they are the only ones too. If you could look behind closed doors, you would see your fear of discovery and pain reflected in the faces of all the others with sexual self-control problems. You've taken a big step by picking up this book and wrestling with the first chapter. If you've gotten this far, you're ready to make major changes in your life. Others on this path have been successful. If they could do it, so can you.

# Chapter Two

# What's the Solution?

## The Causes of Lost Control

You have a sexual self-control problem. You may think you are the only one in the world who struggles so much with sex. Or, you may be afraid to find that you are in the company of naked men in trench coats and guys who hang around schoolyards, or that you might be or become that "pervert." On the other hand, you may have noticed all of the people around you who are stuck in the same rut, making the rounds of strip clubs, video stores, and peep shows, night after night. Whatever your self-impressions are at this point, you are about to radically transform your life.

It makes sense to start at the beginning, so the treatment is explained in this chapter. Then, you'll dive into working through the treatment, one chapter at a time.

### Novelty and Isolation

Problems of sexual self-control are as old as time. Ancient laws addressed some of the same problems that come up today; adultery, sodomy, promiscuity, rape, spying on people who are unaware, and so on (Ruggiero 1980). To have trouble controlling sexual desires is nothing new. The only difference between the past and the present in this regard is that today there are many more sources for sexual gratification and many more ways to establish secrecy than in the past. With new technologies and the modern media, people are exposed to millions more new images than they were in the past. People have come to expect novel sexual visuals and experiences. In the advertising on TV and in magazines, novelty has become the rule, not the exception. The expansion into more spacious living came about with the rise in technology. Generally, people have more room and privacy than in the past. Typically, families do not sleep in one room together; everyone has a private bedroom. Some workers even work at home using their own computers, and never get in touch with other people. They are isolated and often lonely.

*Novelty and isolation feed sexual self-control problems.*

Actions that were once made public immediately (for example, a boy stealing his first porno magazine and his mother finding out about it before he got home to look at it) are now easily hidden. No one sees your pay-per-view bill. No one knows what you do in hotel rooms. Few of your neighbors notice that you come home late at night with messed-up, wrinkled clothes. Few recognize you in the local massage parlor or strip club, and they ignore you if they do. The dance is an old one, although the steps have changed some.

## Sexual Self-Control Problems Are Common and Costly

Sexual self-control problems are as widespread as they are old. Some of the most financially successful businesses in the United States thrive on them. The sex industry offers the promise of sexual satisfaction through more and more pictures, movies, texts, and experiences. People are seduced daily by the easy accessibility of whatever it is that keeps them out of control. Take a look at the following startling statistics:

According to *Adult Video News* (Fishbein 2001), in the year 2000 Americans spent

- More than 8 billion on hard-core videos, peep shows, live sex shows, adult cable, computer porn, and sex magazines.

- More money on sex than all the money earned by all of the Hollywood movies of that year.

- More money on sex than all the money earned from rock and country music recordings combined in that year.

- More money in strip clubs than earned in all theaters in the country.

- More money in strip clubs than on all opera, ballet, jazz, and classical performances combined.

- $150 million on X-rated pay-per-view cable television.

- $175 million on hotel room porn. That's very expensive satellite television monitored by the clerks at the front desks of hotels.

- Over $1 billion on commercial phone sex. Every night, between 9 P.M. and 1 A.M., 250,000 Americans call for commercial phone sex at a rate of 89 cents to $4 per minute.

Sex is big business, a business that takes advantage of your basic human desires. The sex industry is ripping off your time and money.

## Exercise: How Much Money Are You Spending on Sex?

Stop right now and estimate how much money you contributed to those eye-popping figures last month. Take out your pen or pencil again. Challenge yourself to remember every expense, write each item down, and add up all the figures when you're done.

Downloading $ _____

X-rated pay-per-view $ _____

Pornographic magazines $ _____

Phone sex $ _____

Cell phone bill $ _____

Sex videos $ _____

Strip clubs and topless bars $ _____

Hotel rooms $ _____

Prostitutes $ _____

Massages parlors $ _____

Other sex-related expenses $ _____

TOTAL $ _____

## Case Example: Rob

Rob knows all about the loss of time and money. He was introduced to sex by an older boy, and at the age of seven he was masturbating to sexual fantasies about other kids. His curiosity couldn't be satisfied. He fed his growing interest in sex with "dirty magazines." Rob masturbated to images and fantasies several times a day. His sexual obsessions started interfering with living his life. He stopped going out with friends because he wanted to stay home and look at porn. He saw himself as a worthless lowlife. His lack of self-esteem made it even harder for him to talk to people. In his teens he didn't even consider trying to date. With his secrets, he thought dating was out of the question. He got deeper and deeper into porn, because when he was done with masturbating to it, he was left feeling drained and dazed. He liked forgetting about his feelings

Eventually, Rob was no longer satisfied with pictures. He bought one video after another. His nights were taken over by sex magazines, X-rated movies, strip clubs, and peep shows. He hardly slept and his work suffered. At work, he was often put on probation for lateness and his inability to concentrate on the job.

When he was twenty-seven, Rob started dating someone and was inspired to quit for a while. He even cancelled his cable television. He thought he could be satisfied with his partner. A few months went by, however, and his thoughts about porn returned. At first, he was able to get rid of the troublesome thoughts by doing something distracting. That worked for a little while, but his thoughts became more demanding. He convinced himself he could quiet them by buying just one magazine for old time's sake. He told himself it wasn't such a big deal. "Even kids do it," he thought.

But Rob couldn't stop at one magazine. Weeks later he was doing everything he had done before and more. His girlfriend broke up with him and he found himself alone, about to lose his home, and more dissatisfied and miserable than ever before. In desperation, he sought some outside help and was treated with a method called relapse prevention.

*Relapse prevention is the most effective treatment for sexual self-control problems.*

# Relapse Prevention: A Cognitive Behavioral Treatment

*Relapse prevention* is the most effective treatment for problems of sexual self-control and it is at the heart of this book. *Relapse* means to fall back to an earlier problem state, to slip back into old habits. *Prevention* means to keep something from happening. Relapse prevention is a treatment program that keeps people from sliding back into their old ways of thinking and behaving. It is the most effective treatment for sexual self-control problems.

## *History of Relapse Prevention*

Originally, relapse prevention was a maintenance approach added to alcoholism treatments to make them more effective and longer lasting. Researchers at the University of Washington found that alcoholics did fairly well staying away from alcohol when they were in treatment and stayed in contact with their therapists. After treatment ended, however, most alcoholics found it difficult to stay sober (Marlatt 1985). They needed some type of booster program to stay on the straight and narrow path to maintain the sobriety they had accomplished. The idea of relapse prevention was developed because of their need.

Alcoholics need specific skills to deal with the people, situations, and feelings that bring on the urge to drink when there is no one around to stop them from doing so. So, psychologists developed a group of strategies that alcoholics could learn to use *before* they got into risky situations to help them stay sober when those situations inevitably materialized. The basic idea was to figure out what would tempt someone to drink *before* temptation presented itself, and to prepare the person to deal with that risk without drinking.

What the researchers found was that the situations, thoughts, and feelings that got people interested in drinking and losing their sobriety had a lot in common, no matter who was at risk of losing control. The psychologists created a program to treat these common risks. These risks include

- Being in places where loss of control happened before

- Being in conflict with other people

- Having unwanted feelings such as hostility, depression, and anxiety, and not knowing what to do with them

- Thinking unfounded thoughts and acting on them

Out of these early research efforts came an effective program that helped many people to control their drinking over time.

You might be wondering what drinking has to do with a sexual control problem. Dr. William Pithers, Dr. Janice Marques and Dr. Richard Laws (Laws 1989; Pithers et al. 1983) noticed these research successes and wondered whether the program could be modified to help control troublesome sexual behaviors. They adjusted the relapse prevention principles for sexual control problems and began to test how well they worked for people with severe cases of low sexual self-control.

Over time, relapse prevention for what is commonly called "sexual deviance" has gone through many changes because different treatment groups are constantly refining the approaches. Relapse prevention is improving all the time. This book includes the most current techniques, plus some additional material that might not be part of every basic relapse prevention program, but has been shown to be relevant to changing out-of-control sexual behavior.

## Relapse Prevention: The Basics

Relapse prevention is like taking a class.

- First, you figure out what you don't know; what are the thoughts and behaviors that are keeping you from getting ahead?

- Second, you learn what you need to know. Sometimes this involves unlearning information you got in the past that may be wrong.

- Third, you practice what you've learned. You learn to apply your new knowledge and skills to the situations that come up in your daily life. These situations can be actual events, such as having a fight with a loved one, or they can be things that happen internally, like feeling lousy because you've gained some weight and think you look ugly.

With practice, you will begin to feel confident about your ability to control your behavior. It's like shooting free throws in basketball. After shooting a thousand of them, the players get a clear feeling for what it's like to swish the ball through the hoop. They can do it blindfolded. They are in the groove. Controlling your sexuality with relapse prevention can be like that. If you practice the suggestions in this book again and again (i.e., you *overlearn* them), you can learn to maintain control without expending a lot of effort.

## Exercise: The Key Components of Relapse Prevention

Now, get a pen or pencil and take a minute to remind yourself of the three key components of relapse prevention. Write them in the space provided below.

1. _Figure out what you don't know_
2. _Learn what you need to know_
3. _Practice what you've learned_

We are not saying that it's going to be easy. You will have many times of struggle, too. The whole idea of relapse prevention is based on the understanding that relapses happen; that is, doing the unwanted behaviors will happen again.

This program helps people to recognize the many feelings, thoughts, situations, and actions that can lead to a relapse. Then they find ways to change what usually happens, based on their new abilities to recognize these feelings, thoughts, situations, and actions, and their ability to apply new knowledge and skills when necessary.

*Relapses happen.*

This means that people actually learn to avoid relapses by using new strategies *before* they arrive at the point of relapse. That does not mean that you won't have some close calls. Just about everyone who has gone through the treatment would say they came close to relapsing. Some would honestly admit they fully relapsed. Although this is not ideal, it is recognized as the reality of the situation.

When trying to unlearn a deeply rooted habit, it sometimes helps to make a comparison. For example, think about driving a car with a standard gear shift. Someone tells you how to do it. You are taught to release the parking brake, step on the clutch pedal and push it in, turn the ignition key, release the clutch pedal slowly and, at the same time, step on the gas pedal, which puts the car into first gear. It takes plenty of practice to do this and then, once you are moving, to shift gears without stalling the car. At first, inevitably, you stall the car. Or the gears make a horrible, grinding noise. After a while, though, you make some real improvement. Eventually, you don't even have to think about changing gears. Still, there will be times when your skills are sorely tried, and you nearly stall the car—or you do stall. You have to stop to think about how to drive all over again. You might be in stopped traffic, paying attention to the driver next to you. You might be in hilly San Francisco. Every once in a while you might even stall out without even knowing why. Relapse prevention looks at situations like these as hard-to-avoid learning opportunities. The road to change is not a smooth one, but it gets you where you're going.

*Awareness, learning, and practice lead to change.*

# Thinking, Feeling, Behaving, and Experiencing

Difficulties with sexual self-control are problematic behaviors that result from four factors. These are (1) distorted thoughts, (2) intense emotions, (3) specific situations, and (4) the physical sexual drive. That is, the roots of the problem are both inside and outside of you. Research has not yet found the causes of the intense and sometimes unique expressions of sexuality that you and many others experience. It seems to be a combination of causes that vary from one individual to the next. What research has discovered, however, is that when people learn to cope with their emotions, thoughts, situations, and sexual arousal in new ways, they are less likely to engage in sexual activities that are harmful to themselves and others (Marshall and Anderson 1996). This book explains how your unwanted sexual behavior may be linked to each of these factors and will provide many ways to respond differently to them.

## *Thoughts*

In Part II of this book, the treatment focuses on (1) identifying and changing cognitive distortions (otherwise known as faulty thinking), (2) understanding and changing sexual planning and decision making, and (3) knowing what to do with sexual fantasizing. If your thoughts are in order, you will be able to make responsible choices about your sexuality and to anticipate the long- and short-term results of your actions. Challenging thoughts is a key to behavioral control.

## Feelings

In Part III of this book, emotions are another treatment target because they can be depended on to fuel bad behavior. The treatment focuses on learning to tolerate negative emotions such as anger and depression without using sex to relieve them. It addresses your ability to delay satisfaction. In the course of working with this book and doing the exercises, you will learn something about self-acceptance and forgiveness. How other people feel as a result of your behaviors and how that relates to you will also be covered. The ability to experience strong emotions without having to bring sex into the picture is one of the goals of this book. Knowing how to cope effectively with strong feelings is essential to sexual self-control.

## Specific Situations or the Environment

Part IV addresses the issue of how your environment can produce troublesome sexual behaviors. Identifying and avoiding high-risk situations is essential to control sexual behaviors. Masturbation is discussed as a potential safety strategy. Part IV also examines the roles other people play in your life and how your interactions with them can produce the kinds of behaviors you'd like to exhibit. Positive alternative behaviors are also presented.

B. F. Skinner, the famous behavioral psychologist, based his whole program and dozens of research studies on the idea that if you change your environment, you can predict and control what you do. He controlled his own behavior by changing his environment (Epstein 1997). These are tried and true strategies. A changed environment changes behavior.

## Lifestyle Balance

Part V, the final section of the book, focuses on building the kind of life you want to live. It's all about enjoying a life that is under your control. By "control," we mean neither rigidity nor following rules all of the time, although you will probably want to create some new rules for yourself. What we do mean is living your life so that you can manage the ups and downs that inevitably come along without having to lean on sex as your only solution.

Chapters in this section include creating sexual satisfaction without trouble, balancing your lifestyle, and building real relationships with other people. Creating the life you want to live is crucial to managing your sexuality.

*Your thoughts, emotional reactions, environment, and lifestyle can change.*

# Basic Treatment Steps

Some of the essential steps in the treatment are as follows:

- Identifying high-risk situations

- Recognizing seemingly unimportant decisions

- Coping with the problem of immediate gratification

- Combating the abstinence violation effect

- Understanding outcome expectancies

- Discovering and changing cognitive distortions

- Developing a balanced lifestyle

Later chapters will address these key features of relapse prevention one by one. For the moment, here are some brief explanations, just to familiarize you with the concepts.

## High-Risk Situations

*High-risk situations* are circumstances in which a person has engaged in problematic sexual behavior before and in which he or she is most likely to do it again. For example, suppose you get turned on by watching strangers undress. Maybe in the past you spent a lot of money at strip clubs and finally lost interest in the strippers because you knew their acts by heart. Also, you couldn't really afford strip clubs anymore.

You might start feeding your fantasies by trying to catch real people undressing, let's say by watching them at the local gym. Or you might take walks late at night to check out your neighbors through their windows. Or you might get the idea of walking around the local college campus at night to catch a glimpse of someone getting undressed. This could easily lead to looking into windows and, before long, you could wind up going to jail. High-risk situations for you would include going to strip clubs, taking walks at night, and being on the college grounds.

## Seemingly Unimportant Decisions

*Seemingly unimportant decisions* (SUDs) are choices that seem small, but which may lead to high-risk situations and relapses. For example, imagine that you are trying to stay away from prostitutes. A seemingly unimportant decision could be any choice you make that leads you to a prostitute. One example would be making the decision to return home from work by way of the street where the local prostitutes hang out. Another SUD would be going to the ATM (automatic teller machine) and getting enough cash to pay a prostitute for what you like to do while telling yourself you might go clothes shopping, which is something you rarely do.

## The Problem of Immediate Gratification

*The problem of immediate gratification* (PIG) is the term used to describe wanting satisfaction right away and not wanting to wait for different, larger, and more distant rewards. Examples could include having another one-night stand instead of trying to meet someone to have a meaningful intimate relationship with, both emotionally and sexually. Calling a 900 number for phone sex instead of trying to arrange a date is also an example of PIG.

## The Abstinence Violation Effect

The *abstinence violation effect* occurs when someone is trying to change his or her sexual behavior and experiences a lapse in the new behavior. That is, a part of the person's old behavior patterns reappears, and the person uses that small lapse as a reason to relapse fully. For example, if masturbating to pornography leads to having rough sex with your partner, and your partner has stated an intention to leave you if you become aggressive again, you are in the middle of a lapse when you pick up the porn. You are engaging in a lapse behavior (masturbating to porn) that often leads to the relapse behavior (being excessively rough with your partner).

The abstinence violation effect takes place when you think about your lapse behavior (such as masturbating to porn) and you view it as breaking your promise not to do anything that would produce aggressive sex with your partner. You say to yourself that, since you have broken the rule anyway, you may as well go ahead and have rough sex, and in that way you will get the most "benefit" out of screwing up. You view the lapse as so severe that the relapse must follow. But that is not true. Relapse prevention principles recognize that everyone will experience lapses occasionally, but with proper application of the principles, relapses do not necessarily have to follow from lapses.

## Outcome Expectancies

*Outcome expectancies* are what you expect to result from your actions. Sometimes, people don't think realistically about what is likely to happen as a result of what they do. For example, you might decide to download porn from a site that costs $20 a month. In the heat of the moment, you decide that the money isn't important. You may tell yourself that you'll just pack your lunches in the coming week instead of going out.

The problem begins when, at the end of the month, you don't have the $20. Furthermore, you may have forgotten that you downloaded porn from more than one site, and you discover that you are $40 short. The problem escalates when your rent check bounces, and then you are charged an overdraft fee of $50 on top of the $40 you need to pay for the porn. You may get a nasty letter from the bank, and you risk being evicted. Suddenly, that small decision to download porn for $20 a month results in a $90 bill and the possibility of being evicted from your home. Outcome expectancies are about trying to reasonably predict the results of your behavior before you wind up in a financial hole at the end of the month. When you learn to think rationally about outcome expectancies, you learn that you must consider *all* possible outcomes that could result from your sexual behavior.

## Cognitive Distortions

*Cognitive distortions* are errors in thinking that from time to time we all make. There are numerous types of cognitive distortions. One example is minimizing your behavior. You might say to yourself, "I spent only two hours looking at porn last night," when you actually spent four hours; but two of those hours were with your partner, whom you forced into watching it to make yourself feel better.

## Lifestyle Balance

*Lifestyle balance* means having real interests other than planning and engaging in sexual behavior. It means spending energy, time, and money on other meaningful aspects of life. These might include social activities, fostering friendships and romantic relationships, creating an interesting job situation or career, and getting involved in pleasant activities such as mountain biking, or useful activities such as volunteering. Balancing your life will provide enjoyable and meaningful alternatives to sexual activities. Believe it or not, there are great joys in life that have nothing to do with sex.

These important aspects of relapse prevention will be discussed chapter by chapter. The concepts will be explained in several different ways and you will be challenged to figure out how they apply to your life and your specific problems. Then you will be able to practice using these suggestions in your life.

Relapse prevention is a scientifically proven treatment that reduces the odds for some people that they will continue the sexual behavior that's causing them problems.

- Relapse prevention requires that you do the following:

    (1) Recognize problem areas and the thoughts, feelings, and scenarios that lead up to the problems

    (2) Learn many new ways to avoid the problem or to handle it more effectively when it is unavoidable

    (3) Practice new skills

    (4) Balance your life so that sex is not more important than all of the other parts

    (5) Get additional help when you need it

- To do relapse prevention effectively, you must make a commitment to the four Cs of treatment. They are as follows:

(1) Challenge your old thoughts.

(2) Cope with your strong feelings.

(3) Change your environment.

(4) Create the balanced life you want.

# Chapter Three

# Planning to Win

## Making a Commitment to Change

You know you have a problem and you know a little bit about the treatment. The next challenge is to make a commitment to yourself to spend time reading this book and doing the hard work of applying the principles to your life. Of course, there are more fun things to do with your time. Very few people sit around and think, "Hmmmm, should I go out to a movie or work on my sexual behavior problem? I just can't decide."

If you've made it through the first two chapters, you've demonstrated some motivation and commitment to change, maybe even more than you realize. But, just in case you are ready to drop the book and run, here are some ways to motivate yourself to become and remain committed to changing your sex life. Making a verbal commitment to do something has a strong impact on whether you actually do it and continue to do it. This includes finishing projects, sticking with jobs, and staying in relationships. The best way to be sure of your ultimate victory is to make a verbal commitment to yourself or to others.

You're going to figure out what your problems are like and how they have affected your life. You'll be challenged to think about what you would like your life to be like and how it isn't measuring up in certain areas. You'll discover how this treatment looks at your problem, how it is expected to change the problem, the goals of treatment, and how you're going to hit those targets. Lastly, you'll consider the pros and cons of doing this treatment, and doing it now.

*Commitment leads to success.*

# Actions and Reactions

What exactly is your sexual self-control problem? This is a tough question to answer even though you've probably thought about it quite a lot. But think about it again because it is very important to be clear about what you're trying to change. What is it that is somehow hurting you and, directly or indirectly, hurting the people around you? This is not the time to downplay your issues, or make them seem less important than they really are, nor is this the time to deny things you've done that you wish you hadn't done, things that you might even deny ever happened. Remember, this investigation is just for you. What is your problem?

## *Naming the Problem*

Actually, for most people, it's not just one problem they must deal with, it's several. Research by Abel and Rouleau (1990), among the most famous researchers in sexual self-control, and others (e.g., Freund 1990) has shown that people with one sexual self-control problem usually have several of them. One problem tends to lead to another and, sometimes, to many more problems. People who get turned on by rubbing up against strangers in crowded places often report exposing themselves, too. People who make obscene telephone calls frequently have huge piles of porno magazines that they can't bring themselves to throw away. Guys who fantasize about forcing someone to give them oral sex often force others to perform sexual acts they really don't want to do.

*Thinking about and looking directly at your problems are essential steps for this treatment to work.*

In the following exercise, the instructions are to list your sexual self-control problems. Even if you've only done it once, it counts. Focus first on the activities that are causing the most harm to you or to others, but don't leave out any of your troublesome sexual behaviors. That's just asking for more trouble in the future. At this point, it will be much wiser to list them all.

You may be inclined to refuse to even think about certain things you've done. Often, people in treatment have done things that make them feel so embarrassed, ashamed, or scared that they find it difficult to think about them. Sometimes they fear that thinking (or speaking or writing) about their loss of control will cause them to crack up; that if they reveal the things they've done, it will destroy them. These are very common fears, but they are ungrounded.

If there are parts of what you've done that you're trying to keep hidden away in the back of your mind, stop trying. Break the grip you have on them right now. Let the dam break, allow yourself to feel your feelings. Although thinking about what you've done may be extremely painful and may bring up many other feelings, it will not destroy you. No matter how embarrassing or wrong their acts were, our clients have survived allowing themselves to think about them. What cripples people in treatment is keeping some of their behaviors hidden from view.

### Exercise: Name Your Sexual Self-Control Problems

Find a quiet place where you will not be disturbed. Give yourself plenty of time to do this exercise. If you are nervous, do some deep breathing to calm yourself down. Remember, there is no need to rush through this. You want to be as thorough as you can. Now, write down your problem (or problems) with sexual self-control in the space provided below.

My sexual self-control problem is (or problems are)

_____

_____

_____

_____

Writing down your problems sometimes helps to keep them straight in your mind. It clears the confusion. While you are working with this book, you will want to refer back to thoughts you had previously as reminders, or for comparison with later assignments. If you're worried about someone finding this workbook, think again. It's already been established that you know how to keep a secret.

Don't use the fear of being found out as an excuse. Reading this book without writing things down is like watching a movie without sound. You might understand what's happening in the film, and you may even be able to understand some of the words, sometimes, but you'll never get the bang out of it that you could have had. So, to put it as simply as possible, write down your answers to the exercises, and save your work. This is an essential part of the treatment. If you are going to make a radical change in your life, writing things down is your primary tool.

## Naming the Consequences

Okay, you've done the first step. You've identified the problem. Now, you need to think about how your inability to control your sexual behavior has affected your life. Once again, you can't pull your punches. You've got to be absolutely honest about how the problem(s) you identified has/have affected all of the areas of your life.

One good way to think about this is to separate your life into at least five different areas. Some areas important to many people are the following:

- Health

- Work

- Relationships

- Money

- Time

## Exercise: What Have You Lost?

Turn to the "Sample Loss Chart" below and study it for a while. Then, turn to "My Loss Chart" and begin filling in your own entries. Consider all of the losses you have experienced over the years as a result of your out-of-control sexuality. Have you lost jobs because you were late to work in the mornings after staying out late at strip clubs or watching porn all night? Write it down. Have you lost your reputation because people think you're no good? Put that down. Do you wonder where your paycheck goes until you add up the costs of phone sex, video rentals, X-rated pay-per-view movies, prostitutes, sex travel, or porn? Write that down.

*Sexual consequences add up.*

You need to think of the many ways in which your sexual behavior has affected the rest of your life. Lost relationships with friends and family are a given. Loss of freedom is common. Years spent indoors, hidden away from people and enjoyable group activities are often reported, as is jail time. Nights spent breathing in secondhand smoke in bars, clubs, and hotel rooms take a toll. Health problems are routine. Have you lost your energy and vitality because of time spent indoors, never exercising, and the continual stress of searching for more sexual escapes? Don't forget to include these losses in your list. Is it getting full? That's expected.

| | | Sample Loss Chart | | | |
|---|---|---|---|---|---|
| **Work** | **Money** | **Relationships** | **Health** | **Time** | **Other** |
| Postal job gone | $250/month cell phone charges | Mary and the kids left me | No sleep, dazed | 4 hr./day every day | Reputation lost |
| People laughing at me | Can't buy a house | Haven't talked to friends in years | Syphilis | Can't keep up with the bills | Angry |
| No awards | No new clothes | Parents hate me | Overweight, stressed | No time for kids | Feel hopeless |
| Sales job lost | $200/month prostitutes | Alone | Nail biting | Lost years | |
| Embarrassed | Phone shut off | Buddies don't invite me anymore | Sweating constantly | | |

| My Loss Chart | | | | | |
|---|---|---|---|---|---|
| **Work** | **Money** | **Relationships** | **Health** | **Time** | **Other** |
| | | | | | |
| | | | | | |
| | | | | | |
| | | | | | |
| | | | | | |

# The Consequences of the Lack of Sexual Control Add Up

As you get deeper and deeper into out-of-control sexual activities, your losses accumulate. Perhaps you never took an inventory of the costs associated with your behavior before this. You may be feeling a bit shocked, worried, or defeated by what you see in front of you. That's okay. Let it sink in. It's true. These outcomes are a lot to face up to. Even so, this is not the time to start thinking, "Poor me. I'm never going to be able to change." That's what comes up for some people when they do this exercise. They just want to crawl under the covers and sleep until this entire matter disappears. Or they just want to forget about the whole idea of changing and go out and pick up someone for sex. It makes sense for them to want to feel better. That's the whole idea.

But you want to get in touch with the reasons you started reading this book and doing these exercises, and the reasons why you want to finish this treatment program.

If you take the "pull the covers over my head," or the "have sex until I feel better" approach instead, there is a 100 percent guarantee that, if you live to be eighty, you will be living the same chaotic life full of misery that you are living now. Remember *A Christmas Carol* by Charles Dickens? The ghost Jacob Marley had to carry for all of eternity a long, heavy, linked chain that he had created with his bad behaviors. He told Scrooge that the chain Scrooge would have to carry would be even longer than his because Scrooge's behavior was worse and was still continuing. You can think of your own behavior in that way. The chain around your neck will keep growing longer and heavier until you do something about it.

People rarely stop doing their self-destructive behaviors on their own, and there are no magic wands to make life better. If you are waiting for the person, money, job, or other opportunity you think is going to cause you to change, you are waiting for something that is not coming. Your magic wand is doing the hard work it takes to change old behaviors and create a new life worth living. That is what's going to make all the difference. You must resist the urge to hide in the mess you've created and instead use it to make a beautiful life. Remember, wallowing in how sad and difficult this is will not help you. The way to move forward is to identify your losses honestly and use them to reinforce your determination not to add to your list.

## Case Example: Mark

Mark had been in treatment for over two years before he finally admitted the true extent of his problem. He talked repeatedly about having had sex with a couple of teenagers and getting in trouble for it because he hadn't thought that people would see him as a bad person for that behavior. For years, he hid the fact that he had fantasies of having sex with younger girls and had even touched one girl on her bottom while babysitting and became sexually aroused.

He was in treatment, but he wasn't getting the help that would keep him from harming someone else, and he was hurting himself because he wasn't being straight about his problem. He wasted two years that he could never get back because he refused to acknowledge what he had really done. Don't make the mistake of keeping secrets now. Make your list as complete as you can because you will refer to it often during the treatment work you will do while reading this book.

# Dreams and Reality

Now you have an idea of exactly how much your sexual self-control problem has run your life and pushed you around. Even if you can point to a few good times along the way, the results have not been good. The next step to think about concerns fantasies. Contrary to what you might think, it's not the dreams you have at night that are of interest. It's the dreams you have during the day that are important. Your *daydreams* are going to act as a compass for you, and you're going to learn how to read that compass. Daydreams are really the wishes and desires you have for your life. Now is the time to remember what you used to dream of when you thought about your life. Deep down in your gut, your heart, or wherever you feel emotions strongly, what is it that you once really wanted for yourself?

## Exercise: What Did You Want for Yourself When You Were Young?

Think of a time when you were about ten years old. Don't worry about whether you were actually ten or not. Just go with the first event that comes to mind. Can you picture yourself and what you were doing? Good. Now try to remember what your dreams were at that age. Examine this memory to find clues. Maybe all you liked to do was run around in the woods, and you wanted to be a park ranger. Perhaps you dreamed of building things. What did you want to be and do when you grew up? Did you want to travel, to be free? Maybe you imagined being married or having children. Try to remember what you daydreamed about then, and write about those dreams in the space provided on the following pages.

Next, remember a time when you were a teenager. That's it. Capture that memory, stay with it, and recall what it was like for you then. What did you want for your life at that point? We're not asking you to know with certainty. Just try to remember what you were thinking of doing, what got you excited about being alive. What were you doing when you lost track of time? What did people say you were good at?

While you are remembering, some thoughts about sex may start to arise. Try to just notice them and then let them go. Right now, focus on other types of dreams. What kind of person did you want to be when you grew up? In the space provided, list your memories of what you wanted and what you saw yourself doing with your life. If you run out of room to write, continue on another piece of paper. Try not to judge what you write. Even if you think something like, "I don't know what I was thinking, there was no way in the world I could have been a rock star," write that dream down anyway.

Next, move to the present. Remember, this is just for you. What is it that ideally you want for your life? How do you want to spend the rest of your limited time here on earth?

*Dreams
create
motivation.*

Besides sexual satisfaction, what else is important to you? Maybe you have certain career goals. Maybe you'd like to have a nice home or someone to share it with. It could be that you've always wanted to have a child, or to help others in some way. Whatever it is, don't be afraid to write it down. This exercise is not for the purpose of judging yourself. Neither is it for the purpose of pointing out how bad you are for not having achieved your dreams yet.

## My Dreams

Ten Years Old _____

_____

_____

_____

_____

_____

Teen Years _____

_____

_____

_____

_____

_____

Present-Day _____

_____

_____

_____

_____

_____

_____

Remember, you are writing about your dreams because you want to free up your time, energy, and other resources to get back on track and begin to fulfill your dreams.

### How *Not* to Use Your Dream List

One client tried to use his dream list against himself while he was in therapy. He argued that his list was the proof his life had already been destroyed and that he might as well continue to buy porn and take trips to Thailand to have sex with young girls. Clearly, he used his dream list in the wrong way. The whole idea of the list is to open up to hope and new possibilities for your life. If you use the list as evidence that you will never reach your dreams, you're right, you won't. If you use it as a wish list, goals to work toward, you have a real chance of making some of your dreams come true.

## Costs

The next step in this process is to examine how your sexual fantasizing and behavior get in the way of realizing your dreams. How does your current reality mess up your chances for an amazing future? To find the answer to that question, examine some of the consequences of your behavior called "opportunity costs." *Opportunity costs* are resources tied up in one area so they can't be used for something else at the same time. For example, if you are hard-pressed to get to the topless bar after work, you can't go to your neighbors' cookout or get to know the people you work with over dinner. Your time has to be spent one way or the other. If you spend money on prostitutes, you can't spend the same cash to go to a ball game. Having another affair might seem like a good idea until you think of the time you could have spent with your children or spouse. That's time you will never get back.

### Exercise: What Does Your Current Lifestyle Cost?

This exercise will help you figure out the unique costs of your troublesome sexual behavior. Once again, it's all about being honest and doing the work. You've got to get in touch with what your current lifestyle is costing you. Go back to the list of losses you completed earlier in this chapter. Draw a line across the bottom as if you were doing a math problem. Now add up the amounts, the totals, for each category.

For the category "time," try to come up with a realistic estimate of how much time you spend on your sexual behavior every day. Estimate how much money you spend every day.

Look at the number of relationships you have lost and so on. To make it really clear what sex is costing you, multiply the time and money you spend by four weeks. Then multiply that number by twelve months to get a true picture of what your behavior costs you every month and every year. Take a few minutes to complete this task right now. If you need scrap paper to do the math, that's okay but be sure to write the totals you arrive at in the space provided below. That way, you will have a record of your expenditures.

### Four-Week Totals

- Work: _____

- Money: _____

- Relationships: _____

- Health: _____

- Time: _____

- Other: _____

### One-Year Totals

- Work: _____

- Money: _____

- Relationships: _____

- Health: _____

- Time: _____

- Other: _____

## Exercise: What Can You Do to Realize Your Dream?

Now, compare your loss totals to your dream list. Select one goal you would like to reach from your present-day list; for example, owning your own business. Think about what it would take to achieve that dream. How much money would you need to start up? Would you have to go through a training program? How much time would that take every week? How much money? If your wish is for a meaningful relationship, remember, they take investments of time and energy too. Look at the hours you are spending on your sexual adventures and how little time you have left to spend with other people. You never joined the softball league or took the class you were interested in because you spend all of your time and money on sex. Make the comparisons.

Write down what it would realistically take in terms of your time, money, effort, and any other resources to accomplish your dream. This may be the only way for you to realize what kind of barriers you are putting up to prevent yourself from creating the kind of life you want. List at least four things that would have to change in your life for you to satisfy one of your dreams.

**What I Would Have to Do to Reach My Dream**

1. _____

_____

2. _____

_____

3. _____

_____

4. _____

_____

Now, you've identified your problems and understand how they've affected your life. You know what your sexual problems have cost you and how they get in the way of realizing your dreams by robbing you of time, energy, money, health, and relationships. You are also aware of the solution and how it is expected to change your life radically.

## Exercise: Write Your Reasons for and against Treatment

The next exercise is the last one in this chapter. Here, you will weigh the pros and cons of doing the treatment and not doing it. Pros are the reasons to do something and cons are the reasons for not doing something.

First, examine the "Sample Pros and Cons of Treatment" below. You will see four boxes created by dividing the page twice, once vertically and once horizontally. On the left-hand side of the sample you will see "Doing the Treatment" in the top row and "Not Doing the Treatment" in the bottom row. Figure out (1) the pros (positives) of doing treatment, (2) the cons (negatives) of doing treatment, (3) the pros (positives) of not doing treatment and, (4) the cons (negatives) of not doing it. Undoubtedly, you'll come up with many ideas to write in each of the four boxes.

In the box labeled "Not Doing the Treatment" and "Cons," what you have to ask yourself is this: Can you ignore the fact that if you do not go into treatment, your life *will not* change? A year from now you will be in the same misery. Ten years from now, it will be the same. Twenty years from now it will be the same (if you can tough it out that long).

Consider all of your other pros and cons. They are important to keep in mind as you make this important decision. But, we think the prospect of never changing for the better, and probably sinking even deeper into your sexual problems weighs more than all of the other factors combined. It's the linchpin that your future depends on. Refer back to these lists when you think you can't or don't want to finish this book.

Even if you touch on only a few of your negative and positive reasons for starting this program, you will stick with it. You'll soon be transforming your commitment into planning, and your planning into action. Chapter 4 will teach you how to turn your motivation into goals.

| Sample Pros and Cons of Treatment | |
|---|---|
| **Doing the Treatment** | |
| **Pros** | **Cons** |
| No more bill collectors | I have to face what I've done |
| Feeling good about myself | I have to give up affair sex |
| Not having to move | I have to try to make a good sex life with my partner |
| Working things out with my family | |
| No more worrying | |
| **Not Doing the Treatment** | |
| **Pros** | **Cons** |
| I can stay how I am | I'll never get any better |
| I still get my thrills | I will always be in danger of losing everything |
| I don't have to learn | I know I'll get divorced |
| | I'll never see my kids |
| | I'll be alone for life |

## Pros and Cons of Treatment

**Doing the Treatment**

| Pros | Cons |
|------|------|
|      |      |

**Not Doing the Treatment**

| Pros | Cons |
|------|------|
|      |      |

# Chapter Four

# You Can't Run a Marathon on Your First Day

## Goal Setting

You probably already have in mind some goals for yourself based on earlier chapters and whatever possessed you to pick up this book. That's fantastic! Your work will be that much easier as you determine what you plan to accomplish with this program. This chapter will help you break down your goals into memorable areas and manageable pieces. Keeping your focus will be easier if your goals are clearly stated and written down.

Often people tend to think about their ultimate end goals and forget to think about their treatment, living, and short-term goals, which are just as important. In this chapter, you'll learn to view your goals as both manageable and reachable. In other words, this chapter will prepare you to beat your sexual problems and reach all of your goals.

*Always remember why you are doing this program.*

Because there are a number of goals, the discussion is separated into the following four sections:

1. Treatment goals

2. Living goals

3. Short-term goals

4. Ultimate goals

In each of these sections you will become more aware of your goals, including both sexual control goals and life-balance goals. You will learn to detect obstructions or barriers to those goals. You'll also learn how to identify which of the "how-to" sections in this book will be especially useful for helping you to reach and perhaps even exceed your goals.

## Treatment Goals

The first order of business in this kind of goal setting is to make some early goals for doing and completing the program. We call these *treatment goals*. As we all know, it's so easy to let other priorities (or avoidance habits) interfere with what we really want or need to do to meet our real goals. It's like deciding that you want to have a beautiful body. You know that you have to eat right and go to the gym in order to build the physique you dream of. You know what you want and how to get it. The problem arises when you fail to make specific goals to eat right and work out.

*Treatment goals are plans for completing the program.*

Without your "beautiful body" program goals in mind, you know how much easier it is to roll over, sleep for an extra hour, and eat donuts for breakfast than it is to wake up early, go to the gym, work up a sweat, and then cook and eat oatmeal for breakfast. So, what do you have to do to ensure that you will get that great body? *You have to set goals and make plans to follow through.*

Your goals would have to include eating well and going to the gym regularly. You might have to place your alarm clock on the other side of the bedroom, or set two separate alarms when you go to sleep. You might join a gym where you feel comfortable, or buy some new tennis shoes to motivate yourself to go. You could avoid driving past the donut shop in the morning and put the oatmeal out on the countertop at night. You can think of many more insurance moves you might make to be absolutely sure you follow through and work toward your goal of having a beautiful body.

### Planning to Read

In your case, it's molding your sex life into healthier shape that is of interest. What you have to think about now is how you are going to keep reading this book, trying out and practicing the control strategies, and, most of all, finishing the entire text. The idea is not to get through this book just to say you read it. What would be the point of that? If you never consider your problem and never try to use the approaches in the book to change your behavior, reading about it will be useless. Instead, the key is finishing the book in order to reach *other* goals. You will choose those goals later in this chapter. For the moment, think about how you are going to complete reading this book.

Some people get so excited about finally getting some help for their problems that they finish reading the book in few days. If that's you, way to go! For others, though, it may take about a month to read the whole book through, complete the exercises, and begin to practice what you are learning. You've already made it through the introduction and the first three of eighteen chapters. You've only got fifteen chapters to go. You can separate the reading and exercises any way you like, but we suggest that you *do* break them into manageable pieces.

If you try to cram all the information here into your head at once, you won't learn or change as much as you will if you pace yourself. The information has to have a chance to sink into your brain. On the other hand, you don't want to take too long or you'll forget important early parts of the book later on—just when you need to use them. Think of balance. You don't want to do so much at one time that you can't remember what you've read, or that you become tired of it. Neither do you want to do so little that you lose interest and have doubts about finishing the book.

For your first manageable goal, set a reading goal. How many pages or chapters are you going to do in what amount of time? Maybe it will work for you to set a goal of five or ten pages each day. That seems reasonable. Even the busiest person can read five pages every day. Others might want to think about reading a chapter every two days, or about four chapters a week. On that schedule, you would finish in just about a month. Now, work out how you can realistically get to the end of the book.

Enter your reading goal here. _____

_____

Next, think about when you are most likely to read the book, and create your other reading goals based on the current schedules of your life. Be realistic! Figure out your best reading time. Are you a morning person? Do it then. Do you fall asleep at eleven at night? Do it earlier. Now think of where you will read. Is there a comfortable, quiet place you can read privately without being disturbed? It could be at home, in the car at lunchtime, out in the yard, or after hours at the office. Be creative and set the time and place to complete reading and doing the exercises in this book.

Enter your planned time and place for reading here. _____

_____

Okay, have you got it all written down now? There's one more step. *Schedule* your reading time. You might think this is crazy, but do it anyway—because it works. Block out the time when you can read. Five to six? Schedule the time for yourself. If you have nothing else demanding your immediate attention because you saved the time for yourself, you're more likely to do the reading you intend to do. If you pick up the book enough times, you will soon turn the last page.

Set a date for completing the book. Get your calendar out, look a month ahead, and pick a day. Use that date to pace yourself. If you start to fall behind, recommit yourself to reading and start with one page. Then go to the next page, and fairly soon you'll be back on track.

Enter planned date of completion here.   _____

## Planning to Write

Another program goal is to set a goal to do the written exercises. We have already asked you to write down some items. The reasons are simple. First, research shows that people remember things better when they write them down (National Training Laboratories 1996). To stay on track with this program, you've got to keep some basic concepts in mind. If you read about them once or twice and then write down the ideas, you will have fewer problems remembering them when they are needed.

Second, when you have to write something down, you think it through a bit more because not only do you think about it, you have to read your thoughts as you write them. It's like doing one extra review in the same amount of time.

Lastly, once you've written down your thoughts, you have a record that you can keep and refer to throughout your treatment. Even years down the road when you are a master of sexual control, you can refer to your records. You'll know what was happening and what you were thinking about throughout your treatment. You'll be able to go back and remember points you'll forget along the way. And, you'll be able to get back on track if you ever lose the connection between the different steps of treatment. One of the best parts of this treatment is being able to look through those papers when you've got more control over your problem and understanding what you've accomplished. If you don't keep a record, it's easy to forget to give yourself credit for the amazing changes you're making.

## Practicing to Change

The last program goal to consider is just as critical as planning to read and planning to write. For the time you put into this program to be useful toward profoundly changing your life, you must work through the program. In order to achieve change, you must apply all of the techniques you will learn here to your particular problem, and to your unique life. Certainly it's possible that you could try all of our suggestions and not be helped. It's not likely, but the possibility is there. For certain you *will not* be helped if you read this book and refuse to try any of the approaches in it. Since you must do something to get out of your trouble, you are challenged to set a goal to do every exercise in the book.

You will not be asked to do anything that has not worked for others in similarly trouble-some sexual situations in the past. Just think about how all of the methods apply to your problem and *use them at least twice*. It is important to try each strategy twice because the first time you try something, it is always a little uncertain and difficult. Two honest tries will give you the chance to really understand whether a given strategy can work for you. Make it your goal right now to try every suggestion twice. What you put into this treatment directly relates to what you will get out of it. If you do the treatment, success is much more likely than failure.

Think about the difference between reading about hitting a baseball and actually holding a bat and making contact with the ball. Do you think anyone could make a baseball fly across a stadium on the first try, after just reading about how to do it? Of course not. Some skills have to be learned and practiced. Sexual self-control is one of them.

## Living Goals

The next set of goals we want to identify we call *living* or *doing goals*. These goals are really the heart of the treatment program. They will push you in the right direction every day. In order to set these goals you have to ask yourself the following questions:

- What do I want to do with my time?

- How do I want to live?

- What do I care about?

- What is important to me?

- What brings me satisfaction and pleasure that has nothing to do with sex?

*Living goals are what you want to do every day.*

These questions identify what it is that you would ideally like to be doing. Think about what you are doing when you really feel good about yourself. Think about the times when you were really in the groove of life and lost track of the time. What were you a part of then? Maybe you haven't done it for a while. That's okay. It's available to you now.

Your living goals could be writing songs, helping others, learning to cook, playing a sport, and acting loving toward your spouse or children. These goals are up to you. The most important part of these goals is that they be meaningful to you. They have to add pleasure to your life, and they should not come from anyone else. No one else can tell you what is right for you.

For example, it's possible that you might lift weights because your friends think having ripped muscles is essential to the good life, but you are not convinced. You might go along with the notion. You might even sort of appreciate the muscles that begin to appear after a while, but you have no passion for weight lifting. So, you would not include it on your list.

Difficult things are not off the list. Some very meaningful activities are also very hard to do. Try taking care of a disabled person or learning how to meditate. These may be high on your meaningful scale, but they are tough to do. Difficulty isn't part of the equation. It's essential that your goals come from your gut.

## Sexual Control Goals

It may not be easy to think about it now, but along with your living goals, you need to set sexual control goals. Living goals can be thought of as lifestyle balance goals. They are gratifying activities you would like to have fill your life, other than sex-related acts. Sexual control goals, on the other hand, may include behaviors like treating women more respectfully, refusing to tell others about sexual fantasies or to hear about theirs, and, for someone who likes to rub up against unsuspecting strangers, staying out of crowded buses. Of course there is some overlap between living goals and sexual-control goals. Nevertheless, many people find it useful to think of them separately while they put their efforts into creating goals.

## Exercise: List Your Living and Sexual Control Goals

In the space provided below, make a list of five to ten living and sexual control goals. Challenge yourself to come up with a solid list. It's important to make a distinction between the living, lifestyle balance goals and short-term and ultimate goals. With living goals, it is the process that matters, not the end result. For example, if your living goal is to write songs, then your goal is not to write a hit song; it is just to write a song, period. If your living goal is to be helpful, then helping someone to move and then just forgetting about that person is not all that helpful. Your goal is being helpful, period. Learning, playing, and acting loving are all "doing" goals. Cooking ribs like Emeril, hitting home runs like Mark McGwire, and becoming the next Mother Theresa could be short- or long-term goals, but they are not daily living goals.

### My Living and Sexual Control Goals

1. _____

2. _____

3. _____

4. _____

5. _____

6. _____

7. _____

8. _____

9. _____

10. _____

Don't continue on to the next section until you've made your list!

## *Short-Term Goals*

The next goals to clarify are your *short-term goals*. The question that guides these goals is this: "What do you want to successfully finish every day and every week to change your sexual self-control problem?" First, how about focusing on a single day? What reasonable goal can you start off with that will be a step in the right direction? It should be something you can build on. How about something like, "I will reduce my time looking at Internet porn by one hour tonight." That's something you'll probably have to think about when you turn on the computer, but it is possible to do. Another example might be, "I will go straight home after work today, instead of going to the strip club."

The critical parts of setting these goals are

*Short-term goals are those goals you want to accomplish each day and every week to regain sexual self-control.*

1. Making small, doable steps that can be linked together to lead you in the right direction.

2. Making them honest steps—no attempts to stay in the same place forever work. For example, one client set the goal of staying out of massage parlors. This was not an honest goal for him because he never lost his sexual self-control in a massage parlor. His problem was forcing his partners during one-night stands to have sadistic sex with him when they said they didn't want to.

3. Include steps that you know are going to be difficult to accomplish

If you know it's going to be tricky to stay away from certain places where you indulge your sex habits, start there. *The secret is to not take too big a step at once, but to take that small step no matter what.* If you want to stop looking into strangers' windows in the hope of seeing people having sex, make your short-term goal not to go out after dark. Instead, invite a friend over for dinner or to play cards. Think about what kinds of small steps will suit your particular problem. Break it down into small steps.

### Exercise: List Your Weekly Short-Term Goals

Before you write your weekly goals, you may wish to make some copies of the blank short-term goals page so that you'll have blank pages for the coming weeks. If you prefer not to make copies, you can use your journal to create these lists in the future. Now, list seven small steps you want to take by the end of this week, one for each day. Remember, you're working toward a weekly short-term goal now.

### My Weekly Short-Term Goals

**This Week's Seven Steps**

1. _____

2. _____

3. _____

4. _____

5. _____

6. _____

7. _____

## *The Build-Up Approach and the Working Backward Approach*

You can think of setting short-term goals in either of two ways, whichever works for you. One way is to think of what you would actually accomplish at the end of a week of taking one step after another until you have completed seven steps. We call this way the *build-up approach*. Or, you can think of what you'd like to achieve by the end of the week and then break that down into seven manageable pieces, *working backward*.

Let's say you have been having numerous affairs and they are threatening to ruin your reputation, career, marriage, and finances. Think about how you usually create opportunities to have those affairs. Maybe you collect the phone numbers of people you find attractive. It's possible that you collect dozens of numbers so that there's a chance that one out of five will agree to have sex with you. Let's say that for years your goal has been to collect five numbers every day.

Taking the build-up approach to sexual self-control goal setting, you could decide that you are going to make a small change every day by collecting five or fewer phone numbers on day one, four or fewer numbers on day two, and so on, until day six arrives and you don't collect any numbers at all. Then, on day seven you set the goal of walking away from the first attractive person you see instead of asking for that person's phone number. No numbers *and* a reduction in courting sex partners. That would be quite a change!

Taking the working backward approach to goal setting, you could decide at the beginning of the week that you want to arrive at the point where you are no longer collecting phone numbers and you are beginning to control your flirting by day seven. Then think about how you could break your goal down so that you will change your behavior a little bit every day. The end result would be the same, but you construct and choose your own manageable steps for meeting your goal.

This is all about getting used to acting differently and not going back to your old habits, so you don't want to take huge steps all at once. Linking your steps together is the way to go. It's like getting into a cold swimming pool. You could jump in and let the freezing water take your breath away. But you might not be able to tolerate the temperature of the water and you could easily jump right back out again. Dipping your toe in, and then your foot, may be uncomfortable, but you could probably make it all the way into the water and even stay in the pool for a while. You may even get a shot at a volleyball game for your trouble.

Staying in the pool or getting into the game matters. In your life, this translates into making real changes and creating the kind of life you want to have—a life that is not bogged down with problems of sexual self-control. Figure out how you're going to get into the pool and start working with your plan today.

You might be thinking, "But I don't know how to keep from doing what I do sexually." Parts II, III, and IV of this book have many suggestions for how to do it. Right now, concentrate on setting some goals and you'll get help on the "how to" as you move forward with the treatment.

## Long-Term or Ultimate Goals

The final goals to consider are *long-term* or *ultimate goals*. The word "ultimate" has a kind of finality to it, but these goals are not fixed or final in any way. In fact, they will undoubtedly shift and change over time. We use the word "ultimate" because you need to think big to set these goals. No one could accomplish these goals in a week or even a month. They are objectives you will work toward over time, using your treatment, living, and short-term goals to move you in the right direction.

*Ultimate goals are big and take time to achieve.*

Typically, ultimate goals are the ones that people think of when they talk about goals. These aims can fall into lots of assorted areas. Different goals are important to different people at different times in their lives. For example, right now you may want to focus on your career. Someone else might choose to focus on family, spirituality, community involvement, education, health, or something entirely different. Think about these areas and any others that matter to you and see what goal you can come up with that you would like to have accomplished in one or more of these areas in one year. Then, think about what goals you might like to have accomplished five years from now. These may be goals you were afraid to set in the past, because you knew your sexual behavior would not allow you to achieve them. Now it's okay to dream big. You're working on clearing away all of the barriers that have been getting in your way.

### Sexual Self-Control Goals

As you create these long-term goals for yourself, don't forget about your sexual self-control goals. These relate to your other long-term goals and to your overall life satisfaction.

Don't make the mistake of taking them too lightly. It's important to keep your sexual self-control goals clear in your mind as you work through the program. It's all about keeping your eye on the prize. Although the grand prize is to have the kind of life you want to have, that won't come without sexual self-control. What are those goals going to be?

## Case Example: Steve

One of our clients, Steve, agreed to share his goals so that other people could benefit from his experience. He decided that one year after the start of treatment he wanted to:

- Be in a meaningful dating relationship

- Have no negative memos in his personnel file

- Have saved $500 toward a vacation

- Not have exposed himself to anyone for at least six months

Steve's five-year goals included the following:

- Being part of a family

- Starting a business

- Being able to run ten miles

- Having no sex-related expenses (for any kind of porn, phone-sex calls, or fines for exhibitionism)

- Having a satisfying sex life with his partner

- Not exposing himself to anyone for at least one year straight

Steve hasn't spent five years in his treatment yet, but he is well on his way to meeting his goals. He says that there are times when he loses track of the goals he set over a year ago and has to go over them again as a reminder. He also reports that when he starts fantasizing about what it would be like to act up one more time, he rereads parts of this book and rereads the answers he wrote in the exercises for help. He reminds himself of what his life was like when he was out of control, as if he were looking through old photos. He admits that, although he sometimes feels like quitting, he never does because he knows that the alternative to working toward his goals is his old life; and he was miserable in his old life.

Of course, it's important to understand that just setting goals doesn't mean it's a done deal. There's still a lot of effort involved in turning them into your reality.

## Exercise: List Your Long-Term Goals

What do you hope to accomplish in one year? In five years? Think about this for a while. Then, write your answers in the space provided below. Use a seperate sheet of paper if you need more space. Give yourself as much time as you need to list your long-term goals.

## My Long-Term Goals

### One Year From Today

1. _____

2. _____

3. _____

4. _____

5. _____

### Five Years From Today

1. _____

2. _____

3. _____

4. _____

5. _____

# *Don't Hesitate: Write Down Your Goals Now*

If you are hesitating to write down your goals right now, ask yourself why. You may be waiting because you're afraid of not reaching them. Or, sometimes, it's the opposite fear. Fear of living a straight life may come up for you. (Some people see straight lives as boring.) But whatever your reason, two things can be said about what's holding you back.

First, you will never complete a difficult task if you expect to drift to the finish line. It doesn't work that way. If you are not committed to a clear goal, when the going gets tough, you will take the easy path out. You will never reach a goal that way. You will wander around and wonder why you are not getting anywhere. Your goals are the clear voices leading you out of the funhouse of your out-of-control sexuality.

Second, of course you are afraid of giving up your sexual behaviors. They have been a crutch, a distraction, a source of pleasure, and a way to feel better for a long time. It's hard to give up something so powerful that's been such a huge part of your life. You may think you're going to die of boredom. Trust us, you won't. You just have to give other amazing opportunities the space to develop in your life. Your sexuality has been pushing them out of the way.

Then, too, some people think they will miraculously grow out of the hurtful things they do. This is often wishful thinking. There are eighty-year-old pedophiles, voyeurs, Internet addicts, and phone-sex junkies just as there are twenty-year-olds with the same problems. The longevity of these sexual problems is so commonplace, there's a well-known term for it. These sex addicts are called "dirty old men."

Keep in mind that your goals are not carved in stone. They will shift over time and you will create new ones to replace outdated ones. As you make room in your life for activities other than sex, you will find new interests and engage in new relationships that will make your future more different and wonderful than you ever expected it to be. A whole new life awaits you. Set your goals and get on with it. Chapter 5 will take you through the process of how to start and finish making changes with all of your goals in mind.

# Chapter Five

# Just Do It

Best-selling author and poet Maya Angelou wrote a book about her early life called *I Know Why the Caged Bird Sings* (1970). It's a story about a young girl growing up in Arkansas in the 1930s. When she was eight years old, Dr. Angelou was raped by her mother's boyfriend. He was convicted of the crime after a trial that was humiliating for both of them. The next day, he was found dead in the street, killed by someone who'd been outraged by his actions. Maya's blood from the rape washed away, but the experience stained her mind. She stopped speaking to anyone (except her brother) for a number of years because she believed that telling what had happened to her had caused her rapist's death.

## Sexual Harm

You know what you want to do and why you want to do it. The next question we have to ask is *how*. How do you manage to keep yourself from being or becoming a victim or victimizer due to your sexual behavior? In response to that question, you may say to yourself, "I'm not hurting anyone, I just (fill in the blank), and that doesn't hurt anyone, except maybe myself, and I have a right to do whatever I want to myself!" Does that sound about right? That's a fairly common response to thinking you might be hurting someone with your behavior. No one wants to think he or she is deliberately harming another person or themselves, but it happens every day. Some of the hurt is direct and visible while other types of harm are less immediately evident, but they still damage people.

## The Sex Industry

Let's take a look at the sex industry in general: strip clubs, massage parlors, pornography, and prostitution. Your demand for sex or sex-related products like nude photographs keeps the industry rolling in cash. Remember the sex industry statistics provided in chapter 2? Billions of dollars are spent every year for sex. The way the industry often cuts costs and turns more of a profit is by forcing poor people to become sex workers. If you doubt it, check with the Central Intelligence Agency.

A 2002 report entitled "International Trafficking in Women to the United States: A Contemporary Manifestation of Slavery" (Central Intelligence Agency 2002) estimated that as many as fifty thousand women and children are brought to the U.S. from other countries *every year* under false pretenses to work in the sex industry. As many as two million women may be involved in sexual slavery worldwide, according to White House reports (Shepard 2000).

One sex worker named Ines told the U.S. Senate a common story (Boston Globe 2000). She was approached in Mexico by some men who offered her a job working in a restaurant in the U.S. for a "smuggling fee." Once she had crossed the border, she became their prisoner. They forced her to work as a prostitute and refused to release her. Fearing for her life and her family, she had sex with an average of thirty-five men a day, six days a week, for twelve hours each day. She did what they demanded just so she wouldn't be killed. After several years of this sexual slavery, she believed she was on the verge of insanity. She escaped from her captors and went to the police knowing she would be sent back to Mexico. Instead, she was allowed to immigrate legally to stay in the U.S.

**You are fueling the sex industry.**

You may think you're not a part of this. Maybe you have never even thought about visiting a prostitute. But if you frequent massage parlors for sex, buy porn, use 900 numbers for phone sex, and so on, you are adding to the demand for commercial sex.

Don't believe those Hollywood movies that glamorize stripping, making porno movies, and having phone sex. The images you see of sexy people in provocative poses are pure fantasies. Many of the people who posed for those photos were forced to pose. Most women who work in the industry are not getting rich or enjoying what they are doing. They are doing it to pay the rent or to avoid physical harm. The notion that women in the sex industry are sex fiends was created by the those who profit from their labor. The idea was spread to make sexual consumers feel more comfortable. The moneymakers don't want you to think about the harm you're creating with your secret sexual interests and activities. If you actually thought about it, you might not give them your dollars. If you don't spend your money, there would be no sex industry.

It is true that people don't always know what the results of their actions will be. You can be sure that rapist didn't think he would wind up dead for satisfying his sexual urges with Maya Angelou. He never expected to cause a child to become mute either. He wasn't thinking of what could happen in the long run. If it had crossed his mind, he probably thought he could keep it quiet with a few threats, or he might have believed he could disappear and no one would ever know what he had done. He ignored the possible consequences of his actions because he wanted to have sex and the little girl was available.

It may have been hard for you to read the opening of this chapter. Perhaps you're annoyed that it's in the book. Maybe you're thinking, "That's not me, I haven't hurt anybody like that and I never would." That may or may not be true. But don't let yourself off the hook so quickly. People with sexual self-control problems come in many shapes and sizes. The problems vary, but the harm is unavoidable.

## Case Example: Barbara

Take Barbara for example. She's a writer who's been married fourteen years. She and her husband have three children. In the early years of their marriage, they occasionally viewed porn together to spice up their sex life. They both felt comfortable watching it, and they always ended up having sex before the tapes ended. Barbara became fascinated with all of the men and women in the videos, the inventive ways they had sex, and how passionate they were. She wanted the kind of sex life she saw in the videos for herself. She started renting videos and watching them alone and began to fantasize about what it would be like to have sex with other people.

Her fantasy life became so intense that she decided she had to act on it. She thought she would "get it out of her system," and she put an ad in the paper to meet someone for sex. One affair led to another. She started missing her writing deadlines and lost a big book deal. Her kids found her distracted and cold. Her husband was convinced she no longer loved him, and he started thinking about divorce. Her friends dropped out of her life one by one. From time to time, Barbara herself wondered how she had become so obsessed with having the perfect sexual encounter. She became depressed and irritable, worried that she might get AIDS, and was convinced she would lose everything that was important to her. Barbara's sex life was out of control.

*You are supporting an industry that harms you and others.*

## Exercise: How Do You Support the Sex Industry?

Take some time to think about what you've just read. Then think about the ways in which you support the sex industry. In the space provided below, write down five ways in which it is clear that you support the sex industry and thus contribute to harming others as well as yourself.

1. _____

2. _____

3. _____

4. _____

5. _____

# The Touchstone for Treatment: No More Harm

A touchstone is like a home base. It never changes. It's the standard that serves as the benchmark. As you work to change yourself, knowing that you don't want to hurt yourself or anyone else anymore can become your touchstone. You can go to that firm reminder in any season, day or night, and it will be there, the same as ever. It is not affected by how you are feeling or what you are thinking. There will be times in this treatment when you will convince yourself to believe things that aren't true to keep yourself from feeling uncomfortable. At some point you may even deny that your sexual behavior is a problem. You'll be sure that you haven't lost anything because of your sexual acting out. You might even compare yourself to other people and say that they have real problems, but you don't. That's why you need this touchstone. You can go to it when your doubts come up, when you don't feel comfortable, when you start lying to yourself, and when you don't feel like doing the hard work it will take to move forward.

## *Immediate Feelings and Making Decisions*

Sometimes, people think they must feel or think a certain way in order to do what they need or want to do. For example, in the United States it's common for people to want to feel they are in love before getting married. They use their feelings of love to reassure themselves that they are taking the right step (Hayes 1999).

Similarly, people want to feel secure when they invest their money in the stock market. They want their stockbrokers to convince them that their money will be safe and even turn a profit. However, relying on the notion that your thoughts and feelings have to seem right to you in the moment for you to do something may not be the best game plan. For example, if to stay married people had to feel they were in love all the time, the divorce rate would be about 100 percent. In the same manner, stockbrokers will say whatever they need to say to make their clients feel comfortable investing money with them. However, stockbrokers cannot accurately predict what the market will do. Even when investors feel confident and secure when they make their investments, the market can still crash with all of their money in it. How does this relate to you?

Well, it means that if you depend too much on immediate feelings and thoughts as your compass, sometimes you're going to get lost, especially when it comes to sexual self-control. Feelings and thoughts are affected by numerous external factors.

You might feel a certain way when you wake up. For example, you might wake up feeling grouchy, but a song you love might be playing on the radio and pep you up. Or you might wake up feeling fine and a song you associate with hard times might bring you down. Or, you could run into an old flame, someone you haven't thought about in years, and feelings you haven't felt in ages might come up. Or, someone you know could die unexpectedly, and suddenly your feelings and thoughts would be completely different than they would've been if that event had not occurred. As you can see, feelings or emotions are affected by many, many different factors in life, and they can change very quickly.

*Immediate feelings can lead to poor decisions.*

### Exercise: Think of a Time When You Made a Poor Decision

Now, find a quiet space where you can be alone to really think about these questions. Try to think about a time when you made a really poor decision. Then, when you are ready, write your answers in the space provided for them.

1. How were you feeling before you made that poor decision? _____

_____

_____

2. What event brought up that feeling? _____

_____

_____

3. Did you act on your immediate feeling? If so, what were the consequences of acting on your immediate feeling? _____

_____

_____

## Immediate Thoughts and Making Decisions

It's also true that our thoughts in the moment can change very rapidly. Thoughts can be triggered by just about anything. For example, remember the last time you were having a conversation and someone brought up an unrelated topic from out of the blue. You would have never thought about that topic if it had not been brought up. Now, imagine an ice-cream cone. Bet you weren't thinking of that cold delight before we brought it up. Thoughts are like that. They are very changeable and are affected by many events that happen inside and outside of you. When you depend on how you think and feel in the moment to determine what you do, you can follow a flawed strategy for living your life.

## Exercise: Think about Another Poor Decision You've Made

Again, take some time to remember some of the important decisions in your life. Then think about another time when you made a poor decision. When you are ready, write your answers in the space provided.

1. Do you remember what you were thinking about before you made that poor decision? _____

   _____

   _____

2. Do you remember what event or events brought up that thought? _____

   _____

   _____

3. If you acted based on your immediate thoughts, what were the consequences of those acts? _____

   _____

   _____

*Immediate thoughts may produce poor decisions.*

It can be useful to stop and think about what you are thinking and feeling in any given moment. To be aware of your thoughts and feelings is the first step in gaining more control over your behavior. Thoughts and feelings change quickly, and if you don't notice how variable they are, you may wind up making poor choices based on temporary thoughts and emotions.

Treating changeable thoughts and feelings as if they are accurate can get you into trouble by getting in the way of your more permanent beliefs and values. As an alternative, *thinking about what you have been thinking* can help you to see what is really going on in the grand scheme of things. This is a form of awareness.

## Case Example: Jane

Jane often has the thought that people are trying to cut her off when she's driving. Sometimes, about fifteen minutes after getting into her car, she starts fuming because she's convinced other drivers are deliberately weaving too close to her. Her response is to become a more aggressive driver, and then she seems to get cut off even more often. The truth is that many of those drivers are not trying to cut her off. In fact, they don't even notice she's on the road. They're just trying to get somewhere the same way she is. Her passing thoughts about their behavior are inaccurate and her attention to those thoughts creates ineffective behavior on her part. Her aggressive driving interferes with her larger intention to arrive at her destination safely without getting a ticket.

This does not mean you should ignore your thoughts and feelings. It means quite the opposite. You want to learn to see your thoughts and feelings for what they really are. They are temporary bits of information about what is going on inside and around you at the moment. Just keep in mind that they may not be useful because they are not arising from your deeply held beliefs, values, and goals.

### Exercise: Describe What "Awareness" Means to You

As with the previous exercises, find a quiet space to think about this question. When you are ready, in the space provided below, write a description of what it means to be aware. What does being aware mean to you?

_____

_____

## Determination and Choice

Sometimes, people believe that merely thinking about something or having a positive attitude toward it will make it happen. Nothing could be further from the truth. Nothing changes without taking action! The old saying that the road to hell is paved with good intentions still applies. To make something happen you need more than good intentions. You need determination. One good definition of "determination" is that it means being able to move toward your goals without considering how you might be feeling or thinking in the moment.

*Determination is making change by taking action.*

If something is determined, it is already decided. It is going to happen. Moving toward your sexual self-control goals can be determined. You've got your touchstone, your bottom line: You don't want to hurt others or yourself anymore. That means your direction is determined. You can't be thrown off your course by stray thoughts and feelings in the moment. You are always ready to take action.

### Exercise: Define "Determination"

Take a few moments to think about what determination is. When you are ready, write your own definition of what being determined means. Remember, it is not simply a thought or an intention.

Determination is _____

_____

_____

If you wait to feel okay before you do something, you will never do it because change is hard. When you first begin to make important changes it doesn't feel good. Along the same lines, if you've already made a commitment to change, thinking up reasons not to change, or reasons to keep on doing what you've always done, is just stalling.

You can always think of reasons to support what you want to do in the moment. Suppose you want to go running early in the morning and you set your alarm for 6 A.M. When it rings, if you start evaluating whether you *feel* like running, how often would you go? Humans like to take the easy way out. Short-term relief is almost always easier than struggling for the long-term payoff. The Nike corporation has the right idea. As their slogan says, "Just do it." You run no matter how good it would feel to climb back into bed. It is a matter of just doing what you need to do. It's a done deal. It's determined. Your mind is going to come up with all sorts of reasons why it would be better for you to quit or work through this program later. Don't buy into them.

You've already made the very important choice to change your life. You've already put a lot of time and energy into realizing that you need to change; you've faced the fact that you have to give up your bad habits, find some help, and make some moves in the right direction. It's always possible to talk yourself out of trying to change. But don't give yourself the chance. Just do it.

Constantly moving toward your goals by doing what you have committed to do is the key to change. Chapter 6 provides help and suggestions for how to deal with the thoughts that lead to the loss of sexual self-control.

# Part Two

# My Mind Won't Listen to Me

# Chapter Six

# Getting Your Head on Straight

Have you ever watched one of those three-card monte games that hustlers play on the streets of big cities like New York? It goes like this: You're walking down the street and suddenly there's a group of people huddled around a game on the sidewalk. The game consists of three playing cards, money, and a cardboard table that can be discarded quickly if the police appear. The player bets the hustler who is running the game that he or she can keep track of one card while the hustler moves the three cards around on the table for a minute, each to the place of another. If the player correctly points to where the card lands, he or she wins the money. All in all, it seems pretty simple. Keep your eye on one card out of three and win the money. A child could do it. What the player doesn't always realize is that the game is rigged.

Typically, other "players" will be playing when the target player walks up to the game. It looks like they are easily spotting the card and winning tons of dough. But those players are shills or decoys of the hustler. They're just there to increase the target player's confidence in the game, to make it look legitimate. The real game begins when the target player steps up to the table, excited about the chance to win some money. The hustler lets the player win a few rounds to increase his confidence. Then the hustler gets the player to bet more and more money on the game. Finally, the hustler starts switching cards like a magician so that the player cannot possibly win. The hustler's buddies also create a lot of distractions to get the player's attention away from the cards. If the player tries to walk away before losing a lot of money, he or she might be the victim of a mugging a few blocks away.

# Thoughts Are Not Always What They Seem

Sometimes our thinking is like the game of three-card monte. To someone who just wanders up, it looks like a fair game. People are winning money. There is some skill involved, so it makes sense that sometimes players would lose and the game would pay off legitimately for the hustler. It looks like it's just a game, and that the player has all the skill and knowledge needed to win. The problem is that this is a wrong assumption. It's just not true. What the player doesn't know is that the others who *look* like players are actually helping the hustler, and that sleight-of-hand scams are being used along with distractions to ensure that the player will lose. The game is not what it seems.

People live every day assuming that the thoughts going through their minds are mostly true, and that they have all of the information they need to inform their thinking. A little room for a correction or for some new information might be considered if it's a complicated topic, or a subject that hasn't been studied before, or something that people generally don't like to think about. Still, for the most part, if their thoughts are about life in general, most people think they pretty much know what's going on most of the time.

## *Individuals Think Their Thoughts Are True*

People have complex ways of thinking about the world that they think are accurate, but their ideas don't always match what others think about the same issues.

For example, if Bill thinks it's icy enough on the road that people should not drive over 35 mph, and people are driving over 35, he thinks he's right and they should be arrested and put in jail.

Everyone learns how to think as they grow up, learning from lots of different sources including families, friends, neighbors, teachers, books, the media, and so on. Over time, everyone begins to develop more stable ways of thinking. That is, they learn less new information as they grow older and what they've already learned stabilizes into systems. Those systems can be thought of as beliefs. These systems of beliefs are about people, how the world works, spiritual matters, and many other aspects of life. The rightness or truth of these beliefs is not often questioned.

## *Some Beliefs Are Wrong*

Consider the possibility that, among all the things that you have learned in your life, you might have acquired some ideas and beliefs that are neither true nor accurate. In fact, some of your thoughts may be downright harmful and cause you to see the world in a distorted way. This isn't because there is something wrong with you or that you aren't intelligent. It's just that wrong ideas develop easily and people get attached to the ideas they are exposed to when they are young. Everyone has inaccurate thoughts on occasion, but most people aren't aware when they have mistaken belief systems.

For example, when you have the thought, "I can't do anything right," is that an accurate observation? Clearly, you've done many things that were right in your lifetime. So, it's not actually true. It is a distortion of the truth based on your current feelings and how you've learned to think about yourself. But, when that thought comes up for them, lots of people *act* as if it were true. They stop trying to change for the better because they believe that in some way that they can't do anything right.

*Acting on mistaken thinking creates trouble.*

When life is not viewed accurately, the problem can become serious because then you act in ways that are harmful to yourself and to other people, especially when your errors in thinking have to do with sexual matters. For example, you might not be aware of this, but one common finding in the research literature is that men often mistake friendliness from women as an indication that the women are interested in having sex, when, in fact, the women are only being friendly and are not thinking about sex at all (Abbey 1987).

You can imagine the problems this creates. For example, if a woman in the grocery store helps you pick out a ripe melon and you're thinking about how she's going to look wearing nothing but a smile, that's a recipe for a disaster. You might follow her out to her car, but she will give you a dirty look and drive away, wondering why you were following her.

## Cognitive Distortions

People with sexual self-control problems have specific types of thinking errors, also known as *cognitive distortions*, having to do with sex. The good news is that since the thinking problem comes from faulty learning, it can be corrected with new learning. That is, you can unlearn your cognitive distortions and develop new, healthier ways of thinking and acting.

Cognitive distortions are so common that researchers, beginning with Dr. Meichenbaum (1977), have discovered that many people are very similar in the ways that they think about things. It seems most people have a lot in common when it comes to making errors in thinking. Let's take a look at some of the most ordinary types of distorted thinking. While you are reading about them, see if you can think of some times when these types of thinking errors caused you problems. Try to think of some occasions when you got wrapped up in each type of thinking error. It's likely that you'll come up with many examples. It's fairly common to have tried-and-true favorite thinking errors that you depend on.

**Black-and-white thinking:** This is the tendency to view matters as one extreme or another. There's no room for anything in between. For men with sexual self-control problems, women may be seen as belonging either high up on pedestals or down in the gutter. No middle ground is considered possible.

**Entitlement:** This term is used to indicate the state of mind where you believe that someone owes you, or that you deserve something from him or her, or from the world. For example, Mitch's boyfriend doesn't feel like having anal sex with him, but Mitch thinks he deserves to have whatever he wants sexually. So, he visits a prostitute, doesn't use a condom, and risks contracting AIDS and possibly infecting his boyfriend.

**Emotional reasoning:** This error in thinking occurs when an action is justified because the thinker feels strongly about something. The fact that he or she feels deeply is taken as proof of its truth. The thinker believes that because he or she *feels* it to be so, it must be so. For instance, Marlene might be very angry with her children and believe they have done something to make her angry. However, she might really be angry with herself because she lost money she couldn't afford to lose on gambling.

**Jumping to conclusions:** This thinking distortion happens when a person makes quick decisions without any information to base them on. People who use this kind of distorted thinking make up their minds without asking any questions or checking out situations. For example, a man might decide that no woman will ever like him again because he is going bald. He doesn't bother to find out that there are some women who are very attracted to balding men.

**Justification:** This thinking error occurs when people create reasons that seem to defend their behavior. For instance, Kim told himself that he was at the topless bar not because he wanted to see nearly naked women, but because he was thirsty and needed to stop to have something to drink on his way home from work.

**Magnifying or minimizing:** This distortion in thinking occurs when people make a big deal out of small issues or minimize important ones. These misperceptions allow people to ignore the real meaning of an event. Let's say in your annual review at work your boss says twenty nice things about the way you do your job and then mentions one area you need to work on to improve. You spend the rest of the day wondering about what made him think you are deficient in that area, who talked to him, and whether you can fix it. Doubts about your abilities creep in, and within a few hours you begin wondering whether you should start looking for another job. That is called *magnifying* or *catastrophizing*.

*Minimizing* describes the opposite process. That occurs when you've done something big and you try to make it seem like nothing. Suppose that, for the second month in a row, you can't pay your rent because you've spent your paycheck on the Internet. You ask your roommate to pay your share again, and you tell yourself that it's not a big deal because everybody has money troubles from time to time. That's how minimizing works.

**Mental filter:** This term describes a tendency to pay attention to one part of a situation and to ignore all the other information that contradicts that small piece of information. For example, suppose you are at a strip club where a stripper pays a lot of attention to you. She smiles at you warmly, and you think she really likes you. You ignore the fact that stripping is her job, that she's trying to get money from you, that you've been drinking, that she smiles at everyone, that all of the other strippers do the same, and that a strip club is not a dating situation.

**Mislabeling:** This happens when you give a name to something and then act as if the label is true, even if it isn't the reality. For example, upon first meeting a certain nurse, Dr. Penix Sbraga thought of her as "Nurse Ratched" (the name of the mean nurse in the movie *One Flew Over the Cuckoo's Nest*) because when they first met, the nurse was short with her and pretty frosty. It turned out that the nurse was simply in a hurry that day and had not taken the time to be warm and personable. In all their meetings after that first one, the nurse was kind and generous, but Dr. Penix Sbraga always thought of her as "Nurse Ratched" and for a long time did not appreciate her kindness.

**Overgeneralization:** This thinking error happens when the future is falsely judged based on a single past experience. People make up their minds about something based on past experience and don't allow for the possibility that any new experience can be different. For example, you may have tried a treatment that didn't work for you in the past, and you may say to yourself that the treatment in this book is never going to work because treatment didn't work for you in the past. If you thought that, you would be overgeneralizing.

**Rationalization:** This is making excuses for your actions. For example, let's suppose your car is in the peep show parking lot again after work. Your wife sees it and asks you what you were doing there. You tell her that your buddy Joe needed a ride home from work and he wanted to stop to see the show. In a situation like that, when you think that if you aren't willing to help out a friend, then you aren't being a good guy, then you are rationalizing.

**Should statements:** These thinking errors refer to deciding in advance what *should* happen in a given situation and not accepting it when the reality doesn't match what you think ought to have happened. For instance, Ray thinks that if he shows a woman a good time on a date, they should have sex at the end of the evening. His date is not interested in sex because she doesn't know him very well and she is embarrassed when he suggests having sex. She refuses to go out with him again and he becomes angry. His anger came from what he thought *should* have happened on the date.

**Victim stance:** This distortion causes you to blame the world for the things that happen to you. It is acting like a victim instead of taking responsibility for your life. Suppose some guy is arrested for having sex in a massage parlor. When he says to himself that if massage parlors were illegal and women had more class than to work in them, he wouldn't be in this mess, then he is taking the victim stance.

## Exercise: Describe Cognitive Distortions

After reading and understanding the material above, find a quiet space where you will not be disturbed, and in the space below, describe ten of the twelve cognitive distortions discussed above. Note that this is a very important issue, so take as much time as you need to work through this exercise.

Name and briefly describe ten common thinking errors. _____

_____

_____

_____

_____

_____

_____

_____

*Recognizing cognitive distortions is crucial.*

In order to change your cognitive distortions you have to be able to recognize them when they come up in your thoughts.

## Exercise: Identify Some Common Thinking Errors

Identify the thinking errors that produced the following sentences. Use the descriptions above to make your choices. Write the name of the error beside the sentence.

1. "I only touched her once." _____

2. "Why do these things always happen to me?" _____

3. "I feel horny. I have to have sex right away." _____

4. "Janet should have had dinner ready when I came home." _____

5. "I deserve to blow off some steam tonight." _____

6. "I'll have to kill myself if someone finds out." _____

7. "She might be married and busy all of the time, but she wants me." _____

8. "Anal sex is the only enjoyable sex." _____

9. "The guy I met here last night went home with me. What's wrong with you?" _____

10. "You haven't said anything, but I know you think I'm ugly." _____

11. "That prostitute propositioned me, not the other way around." _____

12. "She's just a bitch and deserves whatever comes her way." _____

13. "Teenagers have to learn about sex from someone; it may as well be me." _____

**Answers:** 1. Minimization. 2. Victim stance. 3. Emotional reasoning. 4. Should statement. 5. Entitlement. 6. Magnifying/catastrophizing. 7. Mental filter. 8. Black-and-white thinking. 9. Overgeneralization. 10. Jumping to conclusions. 11. Justification. 12. Mislabeling. 13. Rationalization.

How did you do? If you had any trouble figuring out which error or distortion was which, first reread the descriptions of the cognitive distortions, then reread your answers. Then, try to figure out why you answered some of them incorrectly. Spend a little time thinking about how you might have missed the right answer. Finally, review our descriptions and for the next few days practice identifying the distortions you come across in real-life statements. Pay attention to the statements you make and to the statements of the people you know.

## How to Practice Recognizing Cognitive Distortions

Everybody needs to practice identifying their thinking errors. Discovering these mistakes has to become second nature to you. It may take some time to become an expert at noticing your distorted thinking, so start practicing immediately. As you're going about your daily routine, begin to pay attention when you notice people demonstrating their thinking errors.

1. First, try to see other people's errors.

2.  Then try to catch yourself in a thinking error. Pay attention to all of your thoughts—not just distorted thoughts about sex, but thoughts about any part of your life.

3.  Notice the key words (or phrases) that you need to learn to set off the alarm bells in your head. Words like "should," "only," "just a little," "ought," "must," "perfect," "worthless," "fault," and other extreme terms can warn you that someone you're talking to (or you yourself!) might be thinking distorted thoughts.

4.  If you notice yourself using the same words or phrases repeatedly, write them down. Just keep a scrap piece of paper in your pocket as a reminder. When you write things down, you are much more likely to remember them and to be able to bring them up later, when you need the information. You're going to need this information.

## Exercise: List Your Cognitive Distortions

After you've observed your thoughts and those of other people for a few days, make a list of the top ten cognitive distortions that you use and a thought you have had that is a perfect example of that thinking error. For example, you might write:

*Rationalization:* I didn't mean to break her arm, but she said she liked rough sex. (Don't worry about filling in the alternatives for now.)

# My Top Ten Cognitive Distortions

1.  _____

Alternatives: _____

_____

2.  _____

Alternatives: _____

_____

3.  _____

Alternatives: _____

_____

4. _____

Alternatives: _____

_____

5. _____

Alternatives: _____

_____

6. _____

Alternatives: _____

_____

7. _____

Alternatives: _____

_____

8. _____

Alternatives: _____

_____

9. _____

Alternatives: _____

_____

10. _____

Alternatives: _____

_____

*Know your common thinking errors.*

You can write out the sentences just as they come into your head, as we did in the last exercise. It may be the case that five out of your ten personal examples fall under the broad heading of entitlement. That's okay. Just list them. We all have certain types of cognitive distortions that we rely on more than others.

Once again, when you are through making the list, memorize it. It shouldn't be too tough. These are thoughts you have all the time. You will want to be prepared so that the red flags go up when they start running through your head.

After you've practiced naming your own cognitive distortions for a few days, you'll start to get the hang of it. You may even find yourself saying, "There I go again, thinking I'm entitled." Next comes the good part, the change.

## Exercise: Finding Alternatives

Go back to the list you made of your top ten cognitive errors. Read through your list one more time, just to remind yourself what you've been used to thinking. Now, for each one of your distortions, come up with alternative interpretations or challenges to your original thought. In order to do this so it works, you have to put yourself in the situation in which you had the thought. Think back to what was going on at that time. Your job is to come up with alternatives to what you thought in the situation. It will help the process if you ask yourself the following questions:

- What was the situation?

- What was said?

- What could I have thought instead?

Keep in mind that your original thought was distorted. It was incorrect in some way. You have a pattern of thinking errors that until recently you didn't notice were causing you trouble. Now it's time to consider other possible (nondistorted) thoughts that could keep you out of trouble when a similar situation comes up. Below are examples of alternative thoughts that would be useful for challenging the distorted thoughts in your last exercise.

1. "I only touched her once." **Minimization.**

Alternative thoughts could include the following:

(a) Touching someone even once is wrong if that person doesn't want to be touched.

(b) Touching her may have scared her.

(c) I have no right to touch people without permission, and she doesn't deserve to have someone touching her if that's not what she wants.

2. "Why do these things always happen to me?" **Victim stance.**

(a) I am not a victim. I can control my own life and behavior.

(b) Sometimes I create bad situations for myself.

(c) Maybe this isn't about me.

3. "I feel horny. I have to have sex right away." **Emotional reasoning.**

   (a) I can delay sex.

   (b) Just because I'm aroused doesn't mean I can't control myself.

   (c) I am not ruled by my feelings.

4. "Janet should have had dinner ready when I came home." **Should statement.**

   (a) Maybe Janet was busy today. I don't have to have dinner at the same time every night.

   (b) I could see if she needs some help. Maybe I could cook dinner tonight or we could go out to eat.

   (c) I'm not Janet's boss.

5. "I deserve to blow off some steam tonight." **Entitlement.**

   (a) Having a tough day is no reason to lose control.

   (b) Life doesn't owe me anything.

   (c) I don't have to have sex to relax.

6. "I'll have to kill myself if someone finds out." **Magnifying/catastrophizing.**

   (a) My life will change if people know about my problem, but it won't be the end of the world.

   (b) It might be a relief to stop being so secretive.

   (c) Maybe my friends will support me in getting some help.

7. "She might be married and busy all of the time, but she wants me." **Mental filter.**

   (a) Let's look at the whole picture here. This woman is not interested in me.

   (b) That's okay. The right one will come along.

   (c) Maybe she's saying she's busy because she doesn't want to hurt my feelings.

8. "Anal sex is the only enjoyable sex." **Black-and-white thinking.**

   (a) I prefer anal sex to any other sexual activity.

   (b) Even if everything I want to happen sexually doesn't happen, I can still end up satisfied in ways I didn't even consider.

   (c) Maybe I could think about the other person's likes and dislikes.

9. "The guy I met here last night went home with me. What's wrong with you?" **Overgeneralization.**

   (a) This is not the same person I met last night.

   (b) I could have a nice time with someone without having to have sex with him right away.

   (c) Everybody is different.

10. "You haven't said anything, but I know you think I'm ugly." **Jumping to conclusions.**

    (a) Maybe she doesn't know what to say.

    (b) Maybe she's shy. I could say something and break the ice.

    (c) There's someone for everyone. Maybe she likes me the way I am.

11. "That prostitute propositioned me, not the other way around." **Justification.**

    (a) Truthfully, I came here looking for sex.

    (b) My behavior is under my control.

    (c) I knew what I was doing.

12. "She's just a bitch and deserves whatever comes her way." **Mislabeling.**

    (a) I call women bitches just to make myself feel bigger.

    (b) I don't have to be involved with her if I don't like her.

    (c) Maybe I'm not giving her a chance.

13. "Teenagers have to learn about sex from someone; it may as well be me." **Rationalization.**

    (a) It's not okay for me to lose control. I don't know that it's healthy for teenagers to have sex with adults.

(b) I don't think she liked what I did, even if she went along with it.

(c) Why not have sex with someone who is an equal?

*Practice producing alternative thoughts.*

Come up with alternatives for every one of the cognitive distortions on your top ten list. Of course, you may be way ahead of us, having already come up with the alternatives in your everyday life. If not, get going!

You're already aware of those times when you and other people aren't thinking in useful ways. Remember to pay attention to those buzz words, especially to the "shoulds" and the "justs" as in, "I just want to sneak into the women's locker room at the gym. It's a simple prank I like to play." Or, "I should have at least three orgasms every day." You can practice how you would change the cognitive distortions other people make all the time. You don't have to say anything out loud. When you have a few minutes, maybe waiting in line, practice challenging some distorted thoughts you've heard recently. You'll notice chances to practice every day. When it comes to *your* thinking errors, you'll probably start off by catching them *after* you've already acted on them. That's okay. Everyone goes through that phase when they're trying to learn new ways of thinking. The goal is to get better and better at it so that pretty soon you will catch yourself *before* you get caught up in the thought, and before you act on it. Change your thinking and you'll change the behavior that normally follows.

You can do this. Tens of thousands of other people have learned about these distortions and have worked to change the way they think. Psychologists have even managed to train children to challenge their thoughts effectively (Mischel, Ebbeson, and Zeiss 1972; Mischel and Mischel 1983). If children can do it, you can too.

For those of you who like to skip steps (you know who you are), if you didn't try to identify the cognitive distortions, if you didn't make your list or generate alternatives, and if you're having trouble with either becoming aware of or changing your thinking, now is the time for you to go back and do those early steps.

Also, just in case you were wondering, you will still continue to have many cognitive distortions. You will probably have them for a very long time. That is normal. They are like Brady Bunch reruns. You can't get rid of them completely. Having them is not the problem. The problems arise when you are not aware of them, when you accept them as the truth, and when you act on them. Chapter 7 will show you how to weave together your new skillfulness with thinking distortions and your feelings and behaviors.

# Chapter Seven

# The Ball and Chain

Did you know that donuts sometimes leap into dieters' mouths? It's hard to believe, but it happens. They jump right out of the donut case, pry open the unwilling mouth of the dieter, and are then swallowed. It's a modern-day tragedy really, and no one knows how it all happens. Of course we're being silly to make a point. Sometimes it seems as if lapses of control come from out of the blue. You've suddenly got a donut in your mouth, and you have absolutely no idea how it got there.

## Chain Reactions

We're going to teach you how to figure out this donut mystery. Even though it may seem like loosing your cool and your self-control "just happens," in fact, there is a chain of events that leads to pigging out. And you can learn to identify and control that chain of events.

### Case Example: Terrance

Terrence came to therapy week after week with the same story. He never could understand how he ended up in that humiliating room at the brothel where he knew the prostitutes made fun of him. According to Terrence, "It just happened." One minute he was driving to work and the next he was paying a prostitute with money he had stolen from his roommate. During treatment, however, Terrence learned how to go back in time to reconstruct all of the internal and external links (thoughts, feelings, behaviors, and external events) in the long chain that led to his loss of self-control.

For quite a few weeks, he'd been doing fine, but then he had a relapse, and he needed to examine all of the events that had led to it. Here is what the chain of events that led to his relapse looked like.

## The Behavior Chain That Led Terrance to Relapse

1.  Two days before his relapse, Terrence went to the gym.

2.  At the gym, he thought members of the staff looked at him in a strange way.

3.  He interpreted their looks as judgments about himself.

4.  He felt both embarrassed and hopeless. He felt hopeless because it seemed that he would never feel normal in any of the places he wanted to belong.

5.  He left the gym without working out.

6.  He went directly home without doing his errands, because he didn't want to be seen by anyone.

7.  He thought that if he watched some TV, he might feel better.

8.  He thought it wouldn't harm him to check out some of the scrambled porn on the satellite. He told himself, "After all, I'm not really seeing sex because I can't really get the channels."

9.  He felt sexually aroused and distracted from his earlier feelings of embarrassment and hopelessness.

10. He thought he would feel even better if he masturbated.

11. He thought he needed real porn pictures to masturbate with and knew he could find them on the Internet.

12. He turned on the computer and looked for a site with free porn pictures.

13. He found some new pictures and masturbated until he ejaculated.

14. After his orgasm, he felt ashamed that he had looked at porn on the Internet after having promised himself he wouldn't do that again.

15. He felt hopeless and depressed. He couldn't sleep and tossed and turned for hours, until he finally fell asleep about 5 A.M.

16. He slept through his morning alarm and didn't go to work. He slept all day.

17. When he got up, he felt disgusted with himself and became even more depressed than he had been.

18. He watched TV while thinking all kinds of negative thoughts about what a loser he is.

19. He thought about how no one could ever love him.

20. He thought he would go crazy if he couldn't be loved and sexually satisfied by a woman.

21. He thought he had to prove to himself that he could have sex with a woman and that he was not a loser. He thought that he needed to regain his self-control.

22. He fell asleep, exhausted.

23. He woke up about midnight and realized he was sexually excited.

24. He decided to drive by the brothel, just to prove to himself that he was in control. He promised himself he would just drive by and would not go into the building.

25. He fantasized that while he was driving past the brothel, one of the prostitutes would be on her way home and he would offer to drive her there. Then she would offer him free sex, just because she liked him.

26. He took some money from his roommate's stash and told himself he was taking it "Just in case my car breaks down or something bad happens."

27. He thought he would return the money without his roommate finding out that it was missing.

28. He drove to the brothel feeling excited. No one was outside.

29. He felt disappointed.

30. He thought that, if no one was outside, he could neither prove himself nor enact his fantasy.

31. He decided to go into the brothel to prove his point.

32. He went into the waiting room.

33. The sexy girl he really liked was there.

34. She flirted with him and then turned away.

35. He thought, "There's no way she can get away with that. I'm in control of this situation."

36. He chose the prostitute and paid for her services.

37. She said nice things about him as he had sex with her.

38. He sensed that she wasn't really into the sex and knew that she was lying to him to make him feel good.

39. He tipped her and left the brothel.

40. As he drove home, he felt really awful and kept repeating to himself over and over, "I can't believe I did that again."

41. He wondered how he had broken his commitment to himself and concluded that "It just happened."

Terrence's story is so common, it's sad. It's an ordinary example of how you can end up doing exactly what you didn't want to do. When your personal behavior chain is pulling you and you don't try to break it until it's much too late, then you've gone and done it again.

Terrence didn't *just end up* having sex with a prostitute. It took around thirty-six steps for him to wind up there.

**Many steps lead to a loss of sexual self-control.**

Look at that list again. The length may seem impressive, but it's not unusual for there to be that many links leading up to a loss of self-control. You might say to yourself that you never thought of it that way before. That's exactly what Terrence said. The important thing about that is you *can* think about it that way now.

Since doing these behaviors doesn't just "happen," because they don't just "come out of the blue," they can be prevented. And they can be prevented not only at one point, but at a couple dozen (in this case) before they happen. This is no adventure film where the hero has one chance to save the day. You have about three dozen chances to save yourself from doing what you really don't want to do. You don't have to be a hero, you just have to get the job done right in one out of the forty-one chances you get. Does this sound easy? It's not easy, but you can do it.

Most likely, you're wondering how you can do it. How can you prevent something like this from happening again in your life? First, you have to be able to recognize all of the links in your personal behavior chain. Maybe you never noticed it before, but you do have a personal behavior chain that drags you around until you perform misdeeds just as Terrence does. Now you've got to take the time to identify the links that make up your personal behavior chain. These are the links that stretch from doing something that looks fairly innocent to completely losing your self-control.

Now that you've read Terrence's behavior chain, here's an example of another behavior chain to look at and think about. After you've read it and thought about it, go to the exercise that follows this sample, to construct your own personal behavior chain.

## Sample Behavior Chain

For example, perhaps you had this kind of day:

1. You got up feeling angry with yourself because you woke up late.

2. You rushed to get ready for work and cut yourself while shaving.

3. You thought your boss would yell at you.

4. You thought you looked like a jerk because of the shaving cut on your chin.

5. You ran in to work and tried to pretend you had been there at 8 A.M.

6. You worried about whether your boss would talk to you about your lateness, and what she would say.

7. You started to daydream about sex, which always distracts you from your worries.

8. You went to the bathroom to masturbate.

9. You couldn't really concentrate on masturbating because you were really worried. You thought to yourself that you "just wanted some relief."

10. You thought that if someone else were involved in the sex, you'd have an orgasm and would feel much better.

11. You became annoyed with yourself because you have no one to have sex with.

12. You went back to your office more frustrated than you had been before you went to the bathroom.

13. You couldn't concentrate on your work.

14. Your boss called you into her office and told you not to be late again or you would be fired.

15. You thought to yourself that she was being too hard on you.

16. You thought about making her pay for humiliating you.

17. You thought that you'd like to humiliate her, and then she'd know how it feels to be humiliated.

18. You fantasized about her on her knees begging to have sex with you and denying her. You thought that the scenario could never happen, but it made you get hot.

19. You had another erection.

20. You tried to get back to work and ignore it, but the thoughts of making your boss pay for humiliating you kept coming back all day.

21. You raced home and masturbated to the fantasy, but you were unsatisfied.

22. You thought how much better it would be if you could hear her voice telling you that she's sorry, and what a man you are, and that she wants you.

23. You looked at the phone and flashed back to all of the phone sex you have had before. It was kind of satisfying and you could always get the women to say whatever you wanted them to say.

24. You thought of the cost and remembered the bills you had piling up, plus you were in danger of losing your job.

25. You tried to forget about it and watched TV, but your thoughts kept going back to the phone. You started reasoning with yourself to reach a compromise.

26. You thought that you could afford $10 for two or three minutes of phone-sex; that would be enough to get you off.

27. You made a deal with yourself to call, but to limit the call.

28. You got on the phone with a woman who had an amazing voice. She sounded just the way you like it.

29. You told her what you wanted and by the time you were finished, you had reached your time limit.

30. You were so turned on by that point, that you said to yourself, "What the hell, I'm going to do it anyway, no matter how long it takes."

31. You justified the expense to yourself by saying that you had had a really hard day and you deserved it. You were on the phone for twenty minutes and had an orgasm.

32. You hung up the phone and calculated your tab.

33. You realized you had spent close to $100 you didn't have.

34. You felt angry and stupid.

*Make a chain of the steps that lead you to lose control.*

35. You wondered again why you're in this mess.

36. You promised yourself that you would have more control next time.

That is how you must construct your chain, one link at a time, not leaving out anything important. Each link brings you once step closer to the end. If you leave something out and remember it later, go back to the list of links in your chain and fill in what you had left out.

## Exercise: Build Your Own Behavior Chain

First be sure you've read the sample behavior chain above. Study it. Your goal is to construct a list with as many details as the sample list has. When you are ready, at the top of Behavior Chain No. 1 below, write down what it is you're trying to stop doing. Let's say you want to stop calling 900 numbers. So, you would write, "I want to stop calling 900 numbers." Next, think about the last time you called a 900 number. Think hard. Remember as many details as you can. Be careful not to become lost in fantasizing about it, or imagining how you could have made it better than it was. Just see the situation as it was. Let go of any fantasy that comes up.

Next, go back through the day when the phone sex happened. What was going on? Who did you see? What was said? What else did you do that day? You need to go back to the beginning of your day and reconstruct everything that you can remember about what happened. You should also include anything that seems related.

To give yourself an easy starting point, start with how you were feeling when you got up that day. Write that on line No. 1. Think about what was affecting your mood, what changed it, and what happened next. Lead yourself from that point through your entire day and into the sexual problem. Write down each strong feeling you had, and each thought that related to yourself or to someone else. Write down everything you did during the day. Go line by line, and write down each feeling, thought, and act you had or did that day. Add one link after another; when you are done, that's your behavior chain.

## Behavior Chain No. 1: _____

1. _____  ⇩  _____

2. _____  ⇩  _____

3. _____  ⇩  _____

4. _____  ⇩  _____

5. _____  ⇩  _____

6. _____  ⇩  _____

7. _____  ⇩  _____

8. _____  ⇩  _____

9. _____  ⇩  _____

10. _____    ⇩   _____
11. _____    ⇩   _____
12. _____    ⇩   _____
13. _____    ⇩   _____
14. _____    ⇩   _____
15. _____    ⇩   _____
16. _____    ⇩   _____
17. _____    ⇩   _____
18. _____    ⇩   _____
19. _____    ⇩   _____
20. _____    ⇩   _____
21. _____    ⇩   _____
22. _____    ⇩   _____
23. _____    ⇩   _____
24. _____    ⇩   _____
25. _____    ⇩   _____
26. _____    ⇩   _____
27. _____    ⇩   _____
28. _____    ⇩   _____
29. _____    ⇩   _____
30. _____    ⇩   _____
31. _____    ⇩   _____
32. _____    ⇩   _____
33. _____    ⇩   _____
34. _____    ⇩   _____
35. _____    ⇩   _____
36. _____    ⇩   _____

## Become Familiar with the Links in Your Behavior Chain

After you've completed your behavior chain, the next step is to become very familiar with those links. You need to know those links like you've never known anything before. This is one of the most important parts of this treatment. Successful sexual controllers know their behavior chains inside and out.

Our clients bring their behavior chains to every session because they know they are essential to successful treatment. Review yours a few times. Notice how one step follows another. Memorize the general layout. Then, *make another one*. That's right. Once you've made one behavior chain and memorized the links as best you can, then it's time to do another one.

### Exercise: Make a Second Behavior Chain

For your second behavior chain, think of another time when you lost your sexual self-control. This problem may have something in common with the problem you used for your first chain, but the specific example you use should be based on a different situation. Remember to name the problem you would like to control at the top of the page. Then once again think back to what got you wrapped up in that chain. Think of how you were doing when you awoke on that day and go on from there. It can be helpful to think of the first thing that happened that day that made you angry or unhappy and then to move down the chain, listing events, thoughts, and feelings one by one.

It's important to do two behavior chains. You should do a second one because only then can you start to see patterns in your behavior. You will observe how there is a kind of blueprint you generally follow that leads to your loss of control. The details might be a little different from one experience to another, but the general model is often the same. For a lot of people, their chains always contain the same general motivations, such as feeling bad, wanting to be distracted or to feel better, fantasizing, proving a point, making sex more exciting, or finding a substitution for love or for some types of sex. Make a second behavior chain to reconstruct exactly what you did when you lost your sexual self-control another time. Then compare the two behavior chains to discover some of your motivations and common ways of acting.

## Behavior Chain No. 2: _____

1. _____  ⇩  _____

2. _____  ⇩  _____

3. _____  ⇩  _____

4. _____  ⇩  _____

5. _____  ⇩  _____

6. _____  ⇩  _____

7. _____  ⇩  _____

8. _____  ⇩  _____

9. _____  ⇩  _____

10. _____  ⇩  _____

11. _____  ⇩  _____

12. _____  ⇩  _____

13. _____  ⇩  _____

14. _____  ⇩  _____

15. _____  ⇩  _____

16. _____  ⇩  _____

17. _____  ⇩  _____

18. _____  ⇩  _____

19. _____  ⇩  _____

20. _____  ⇩  _____

21. _____  ⇩  _____

22. _____  ⇩  _____

23. _____  ⇩  _____

24. _____  ⇩  _____

25. _____  ⇩  _____

26. _____  ⇩  _____

27. _____  ⇩  _____

28. _____  ⇩  _____

29. _____  ⇩  _____

30. _____ ⇩ _____

31. _____ ⇩ _____

32. _____ ⇩ _____

33. _____ ⇩ _____

34. _____ ⇩ _____

35. _____ ⇩ _____

36. _____ ⇩ _____

### Exercise: What I've Learned from My Behavior Chains

Before you do anything else, answer the following three questions:

1. What starts the chain for you? _____

2. What keeps you going down the chain? _____

_____

_____

3. What's usually your point of no return (the point where you can't resist what you are about to do)? _____

_____

_____

If you answered the questions in the exercise above honestly, you are that much further down the road to understanding and solving your problems.

# Learning to Recognize When You Are Building Links in Your Chain

*Memorize and compare your chains.*

After you have identified the links in your chain and are really familiar with them, you are ready to go on to the next step. Sitting down and writing out the details of your chain is one thing, but recognizing the chain *when you are in the middle of connecting one link to the next* is another. You have to begin to tune into your thoughts, feelings, and actions as you never have before.

Sometimes a person's state of awareness can be compared to a radio frequency. A lot of the time, we walk around in the static zone. No signals get through to us. We're not paying attention to how we're feeling, what we're thinking, or what we are doing. We're just living in the chaos. Real change requires us to live life differently, to live life aware. We have to observe our patterns of feeling, thinking, and acting while they are happening. Forget about simply looking back and seeing what you did wrong. No more of that. That's not good enough for you anymore. You've got to notice this business *while* it is happening. You've learned the parts of your chain. You know the major obstacles on the chain. The next thing you have to do is associate them with warning bells and red flags.

**Paying attention to your behavior patterns is vital to changing them.**

When you start feeling bad, feeling horny, feeling you deserve sex (or whatever is part of your chain), warning bells have to go off. Danger, danger!! Now that you know what the signs are that tell you you're on your way to losing control, it's not going to be as easy to ignore them as it was in the past. Still, some people surprise us. They try to pretend they never learned these skills and go on to lose control anyway. That can't be you. Tune yourself into your warning signals. You'll be amazed how clear the signals can become.

We said that you have about thirty-six chances to prevent your problematic sexual behavior from happening, and we weren't kidding. The next step in changing your behavior for good is to examine each link on your chain and come up with alternatives or safety actions. *Alternatives* or *safety actions* (also called *coping responses*) are ways to get out of the chain when you are caught in it. They are ways to free yourself from becoming tangled up in the chain.

You know that your chain leads to disaster, and you know you have to do something different so that you never reach the end of the chain again. An alternative is something you do *instead* of your usual response in a situation. An alternative makes it possible for you to think and behave in a different way than you did before.

**Safety actions release you from your chain.**

First, you have to come up with some good alternatives for yourself. Take one of your chains. Look at one of the links or steps in the chain. You felt, thought, or did something. What was it? We're not going to ask you to do anything with any feelings that are on your chain. Feelings come and feelings go. You can't do much about how you are feeling and we don't want you to try. Just notice that how you feel affects how you think and what you do at a given time.

You can't really change your feelings very well, but you can become aware of them and how they affect the other parts of your life. What you can change directly is how you think about things and what you do about them. Let's turn to the parts of the chain that are composed of thoughts and actions. They probably make up many of the links in your chain.

### Exercise: What to Do with Your Thoughts in Your Behavior Chain

In the space provided below, list every thought on your chain. In chapter 6, you practiced coming up with alternative thoughts. You should be pretty good at it by now. Go for it. For every thought on your chain, come up with alternatives and write them in. Create more than one alternative. That will give you more ways to escape when these thoughts appear. Go through your whole chain, replacing the thoughts that led you down that dark sexual road with better alternatives. This will take you a little while. Don't rush through it. Come up with as many alternatives as you can. If you need more space, write on a separate sheet of paper or in your journal.

## Behavior Chain Thoughts and Alternatives

1. _____

Alternatives: _____

_____

2. _____

Alternatives: _____

_____

3. _____

Alternatives: _____

_____

4. _____

Alternatives: _____

_____

5. _____

Alternatives: _____

_____

6. _____

Alternatives: _____

_____

7. _____

Alternatives: _____

_____

8. _____

Alternatives: _____

_____

9. _____

Alternatives: _____

_____

10. _____

Alternatives: _____

_____

## Exercise: What to Do with Your Actions in Your Behavior Chain

Next, look at the actions on your chain, those things you did that took you closer to the end of your chain. Again, come up with realistic alternatives. If stopping at a bar led you down the destructive path, what could you have done instead? Think of lots of options, particularly options that are appealing. Maybe you could have biked to a friend's house, visited a local coffeehouse, called someone, played with your children, watched a movie, walked in the park, visited a mall and shopped or watched the people, done some yard work or housework, cooked a meal, or any one of thousands of other alternatives.

Part V will address developing new interests and reclaiming activities you used to like before you became obsessed with sex. You can skip ahead and take a look at those suggestions if you'd like. For now, whatever activities you choose as alternatives are okay as long as they are not linked to sexual misbehavior. It's important that you do something different that doesn't lead you down the same lousy trail or to another dangerous path. At this point, you've been dealing with your problems for a while. You may not have liked to name them in the past, but you've got an excellent idea of the actions that cause you to lose control. It's time to admit to them and change the way you're living. Does that mean you'll never be able to go into a bar again if bars are on your chain? Maybe not. It does mean that you can't go into a bar for a long while, at least until going to a bar is no longer associated with the rest of your behavior chain.

Right about now you might be thinking that you're being asked to give up too much. But this discussion began with the question of how you can get rid of your problematic sexual behavior. And here we are saying that maybe you should stop going to bars and clubs. That's because the part of their chains that always confuses people is that many of their links don't look sexual at all. Many of the links look as if they have nothing whatsoever to do with sex, and for other people, there may not be any relationship between a specific link and sex. However, *you* have created a powerful association between these activities and sex where others have not made that connection. They are sexual because you made them sexual. For example, keeping a certain sum of money in a wallet is a perfectly normal activity for most people. For Karen, however, having the right amount money in her wallet allows her to pick up one-night stands after work. Having the money in her wallet is a link in her behavior chain.

Now, go to your behavior chains and, in the space provided below, list every action in your chain and write in some alternative behaviors. Learn them and *start practicing the alternatives*. Replace your chain habits with new ones again and again. When your car starts heading for the bar or the ATM, back it up and go somewhere else, preferably someplace that is also fun for you.

## Behavior Chain Actions and Alternatives

1. _____

Alternatives: _____

_____

2. _____

Alternatives: _____

_____

3. _____

Alternatives: _____

_____

4. _____

Alternatives: _____

_____

5. _____

Alternatives: _____

_____

6. _____

Alternatives: _____

_____

7. _____

Alternatives: _____

_____

8. _____

Alternatives: _____

_____

9. _____

Alternatives: _____

_____

10. _____

Alternatives: _____

_____

Make a brief list of your alternatives and keep it in your wallet so you'll have a small reminder of what to do if you run into trouble. If you're saying to yourself that the nonsexual steps on the chain have nothing to do with your problem, you are wrong. You have to change them to change your sexual behavior. You have nearly forty chances to exit your chain before the worst happens. You change one thought, and you're off the chain. You change one action, you're off the chain. Learn to take these golden opportunities to do something better with your life.

A word to the wise: if you find yourself at a link on your chain and your mind starts trying to make a deal (as in, "just this once," "never again," "I promise I won't go too far"), take out your list of alternatives from your wallet and do one alternative right away. Unfortunately, our minds like to keep life at a standstill. They don't like change. Don't let your mind convince you that you can handle a slip. It's like releasing a kid in a candy shop. The kid might leave without the chocolate, but what are the chances? As the old saying goes, we can resist anything but temptation. Chapter 8 will teach you what to do when the decision-making process gets tricky.

*Learn and practice alternative behaviors.*

# Chapter Eight

# The Matrix versus the Problem of Immediate Gratification

## Decision Making and Self-Control

Is there anything in the world that knocks you off your feet the way an orgasm does? Orgasm has been called the "little death," because for a few moments, you feel suspended between life and death. Your mind and body are released in an explosion of feeling, and nothing else seems to matter. Nothing else comes to mind. Orgasm offers the promise of a few moments of freedom and pleasure that are difficult to grasp in any other way. It's true that some people report having felt similar rushes and the sense of freedom from experiences like meditation, flying, or communing with nature, but these are not instant, knock-you-out sorts of experiences. Drug use may come closer to the mental effect of orgasm, but it doesn't offer the physical relief that is such an appealing part of the package, and you have to contend with the nasty aftereffects. There's pretty much nothing that competes with a good, old-fashioned orgasm. This is part of the problem.

# The Problem of Immediate Gratification

When something so powerful and satisfying is within reach, you stretch out your hand to grab it over and over again. It's almost automatic. It's a no-brainer; you don't really think about it. You want immediate satisfaction and the satisfaction is easy to access, so you go for it. You focus on the hot aspects of whatever is tantalizing you.

*Seeking quick satisfaction leads to loss of control.*

This is what researchers in this area call "the PIG" (Laws 1989). The PIG stands for the Problem of Immediate Gratification. It's the problem of going after what you want in the moment that you want it and not considering what it might cost you. The pig image sort of fits. If you've ever seen pigs going after food, you know it's not pretty. They stuff themselves from the moment the slop is served until it's gone. For people with problems of sexual self-control, feeding the PIG is a major factor in their loss of self-control. The PIG is really about not considering the results or consequences of decisions made in the moment.

Think about it. If you reach the moment where you have to control yourself or have an orgasm, what do you do? You go for the orgasm. You may become obsessed with the orgasm. You don't even give yourself the opportunity to get involved in making a decision about what would be the best thing for you to do, especially in the long run. Instead, your hormones are raging, your mind is on hold, and sometimes you'd like to keep it that way. You want immediate gratification and you don't want anything to get in the way.

## Basic Principles of Self-Control

The need or desire for immediate satisfaction has been researched with children. Dr. Walter Mischel (1983), a famous psychologist who specialized in issues of self-control, found that if you offer children three marshmallows to be eaten immediately, or five marshmallows if they wait for a few minutes, many children will eat the three marshmallows right away, especially if they haven't been taught how to delay, or put off, being satisfied. Mischel found that the kids who can't control their need for immediate gratification in childhood lead less successful lives in their teenage and adult years. They have more problems in school and at work, and fewer friends.

The good news is that you can learn how to wait for gratification. You can learn to wait for the long-term payoff. By taking the route of immediate gratification (the sex), you are missing out on the long-term benefits of *not* taking it. The even better news is that, typically, the short-term payoff is smaller than the long-term payoff.

*Long-term benefits are lost in short-term fixes.*

You might have an orgasm if you choose the short-term payoff, but if you wait for the long-term satisfaction of delaying it, you might gain the long-term benefits of not losing your money or time pursuing the orgasm or being able to tend to other parts of your life, such as building a strong, intimate relationship and thus having regular access to lots of orgasms. Also, you will reduce your stress by not having to worry about getting into trouble with family, friends, or the law, and you will improve your sexual health.

You can look at it still another way: If you go for the orgasm, you're trading a short-term fix for long-term misery. You can have the bigger reward if you are able to reason with yourself in the moment. People do this all the time. They go to school for years, not making any money in the hope of making more money than they would if they had taken a job right out of high school. Some people don't eat sweets in the hope of losing weight. Some drive junker cars so they can pay for their kids' education or take a great vacation someday.

The key is to distance yourself from the hot, emotional, tempting pull of sex. You want to make cool, rational choices. Dr. Mischel and colleagues (1972) demonstrated that if you focus on the hot, tempting aspects of your choice, you're more likely to lose control than if you focus on the cool, boring parts of whatever is tempting you. When the kids in the study focused on the shape of the marshmallows instead of the taste, they succeeded in not eating them right away. They were able to better control themselves. When you focus on how you will spend your free time with friends, films, sports, or computers, instead of focusing exclusively on orgasm or other aspects of sex, you will be better able to control yourself. You want to take the steam out of the engine.

## Exercise: My Problem of Immediate Gratification

In the space below, using your own words, describe what the problem of immediate gratification is. Then list the most tantalizing parts of your sexual temptations. Which aspects of your typical sexual situations influence and pull you to move toward orgasm and lessen your self-control? On the same line, next to each of these influences or pulls, there is space for you to write down an alternative focus.

For example, a hot thought might be concentrating on a sexy voice. A cool alternative would be to pay attention to the fact that you are talking to someone you don't know (and probably wouldn't even like in person) on the telephone in your unsexy kitchen. Remember to pay attention to the cool aspects of the person or situation, those aspects that do not lead you closer to orgasm, but instead lessen your arousal and interest in being sexual. This is a skill you can use to combat the problem of immediate gratification.

The problem of immediate gratification is _____

_____

_____

_____

Hot Aspects of My Sexual Situations          Cool Aspects of My Sexual Situations

———————————————————          ———————————————————

———————————————————          ———————————————————

———————————————————          ———————————————————

———————————————————          ———————————————————

———————————————————          ———————————————————

———————————————————          ———————————————————

———————————————————          ———————————————————

Making the decision not to feed the PIG requires a little advance work, but once you learn how to do it, it becomes easier. And, like anything else, the more you practice, the better you'll get at it. When you learn to think about your thoughts, you're breaking out of the grip your primitive instincts have over you. This is what differentiates us from the pigs in the world. Animals don't have the ability to be self-aware or to think about their thinking, because they don't have a complex language as humans have. They can't remind themselves to pick up milk on the way home by repeating to themselves, "Don't forget the milk, don't forget the milk." Animals acts are mostly based on instinct. Luckily, humans have the ability to think on a higher level. That is, humans can think about thinking. People can consider whether what they are thinking about is good for them. We can weigh the positives and negatives before we act.

*Before acting, consider what the results are likely to be.*

## The Decision Matrix

A *decision matrix* is a way of figuring out the long- and short-term costs and benefits of doing something. Good decisions are those in which the expected benefits are greater than the expected costs. Making good decisions about sex is a must in the battle to resist sexual trouble. For our purposes, the decision matrix is a chart that is filled in with both the immediate and long-term (delayed) costs and benefits of (1) losing control and (2) not losing control. When completing your decision matrix, there are three areas to consider:

1. Short-term goals versus long-term goals

2. Losing control versus not losing control

3. Costs and benefits

| Sample Decision Matrix | | | | |
|---|---|---|---|---|
| | **Short Term** | | **Long Term** | |
| | Benefits | Costs | Benefits | Costs |
| **Losing Control** | Having an orgasm<br>Relieving tension | Risking arrest<br>Spending money I don't have<br>Risking AIDS<br>Feeling dirty<br>Risking my family | I don't have to change<br>I can still get my kicks in the same way | I could get an STD<br>I could lose everything<br>I'll never be able to buy a house<br>I could spend time in prison |
| **Not Losing Control** | I don't have to worry so much<br>I can put my attention on other things like my job<br>I could go camping again<br>I'd have some money in my pocket<br>I could take my wife out and show her I love her | I'd have to wait to be sexually satisfied<br>I might feel frustrated<br>I won't know how to distract myself | I could have some respect for myself<br>People might learn to love me<br>I could start my own business and stop working for other people<br>Maybe I could have a kid like I wanted to | I might be boring |

Look at the chart of a sample decision matrix above. There are five columns. The column on the extreme left is labeled "Losing Control" on the top half of the chart and "Not Losing Control" on the bottom half. Next to that column, still on the left-hand side, there are two columns under the heading "Short Term." One column shows the benefits and the other column shows the costs for losing control and not losing control in the short term. Similarly, on the right-hand side, under the heading "Long Term," there are two columns that show the long-term benefits and costs of losing control and not losing control.

In the short term, losing control has some benefits and some costs. In the long term, losing control also has some benefits and some costs. Similarly, not losing control has both benefits and costs in both the short term and the long term.

To work with this decision matrix, you must consider the following eight questions:

1. What are the *benefits* of losing control in the *short term*?

2. What are the *costs* of losing control in the *short term?*

3. What are the *benefits* of losing control in the *long term?*

4. What are the *costs* of losing control in the *long term?*

5. What are the *benefits* of *not losing control* in the *short term?*

6. What are the *costs* of *not losing control* in the *short term?*

7. What are the *benefits* of *not losing control* in the *long term?*

8. What are the *costs* of *not losing control* in the *long term?*

*Understand how to construct a decision matrix.*

In our example, you will see that, for this person, the short-term *benefits* of losing control are "Having an orgasm" and "Relieving tension." Then we move to the column to the right, and we ask the second question, "What are the short-term *costs* of losing control?" For our sample decision matrix, the answers are: "Risking arrest," "Spending money I don't have," "Risking AIDS," "Feeling dirty," and "Risking my family." When we ask the third question, "What are the long-term benefits of losing control," we see "I don't have to change" and "I can still get my kicks in the same way." The fourth question about the long-term costs of losing control is answered with "I could get an STD," "I could lose everything," "I'll never be able to buy a house," and "I could spend time in prison." Then we move to the bottom half of the chart and repeat the process, asking the questions numbered 5 through 8, only this time we are concerned with finding out the short- and long-term benefits and costs of *not losing control.*

What you will find is that sometimes the benefits in one column are the same as the costs in another column. Read through the whole sample matrix and be sure you understand how to construct it.

## Exercise: Construct Your Own Sexual Decision Matrix

Now, it's time for you to create your own sexual decision matrix. This will take some time to do. Make sure you have a quiet place in which to work and that you will not be disturbed. Remember that this matrix is about harmful sexual behavior. Concentrate on one column at a time. Fill in as many costs and benefits as you can think of. Move from column to column until all of the benefits and costs have been filled in for "Losing Control" and for "Not Losing Control." Great job!

When you have finished, you will have put down on paper exactly what you will face in the near and distant future if you continue to indulge in your sexual behavior. You also have a pretty good idea of what's in store for you if you can stop doing the sexual practices that get you into trouble. When it's staring you in the face, it's not so easy to ignore the consequences of continuing your out-of-control sexual behaviors or to ignore the benefits of sexual self-control. The long-term costs of doing the behavior and the long-term benefits of not doing it always outweigh the immediate payoff of having that orgasm.

| My Sexual Decision Matrix | | | | |
|---|---|---|---|---|
| | **Short Term** | | **Long Term** | |
| | Benefits | Costs | Benefits | Costs |
| **Losing Control** | | | | |
| **Not Losing Control** | | | | |

The problem is that an orgasm is so tempting and immediate that you don't think about what will come later (sometimes on purpose). People sometimes say, "I didn't think," to excuse their bad behavior and to make themselves feel better. It makes no sense. If you want to really feel good, don't do the sex in the first place. Avoiding the negative consequences of bad behavior always beats feeling sorry after the deeds are done.

*Make yourself think of what can happen.*

This decision matrix is your own personal cheat sheet that you can use to remind yourself of the long-term and short-term costs of your behavior. Sometimes, stopping a behavior chain before someone gets hurt is mainly a matter of realizing what can happen if you continue doing it. Most people tend to ignore long-term consequences and focus on short-term benefits. Who hasn't broken the speed limit to get somewhere faster only to wind up paying high-cost speeding fines and higher insurance premiums later on? The problem is that these long-term costs create misery for you, and probably for those around you. Ignoring the long-term cost of anything is rarely to our benefit, and it is especially harmful when it comes to sex.

## Copy Your Decision Matrix

Some people like to carry a copy of their decision matrix with them at all times. This is a great idea. They make a small version, about the size of a business card, to keep in a wallet. It can even be laminated so that it doesn't get worn out. Laminated (put in plastic) or not, having that card with you at all times can be like having a safety cushion on an airplane. You sit on it and don't even think about it until there's some turbulence. If the plane starts bucking, that cushion instantly becomes your best friend. Get to know *your* new best friend, the decision matrix. You can use the matrix approach for making decisions in any area, but especially for choices related to your sexual problems.

*A decision matrix is a decision-making helper.*

## Smart Ways to Use the Matrix

For example, drinking might be an activity that typically leads to sexual trouble for you. Instead of focusing on the ultimate loss of sexual control in your matrix, you can focus on an earlier step in your behavior chain (drinking) and break the chain before you go too far. You can use the matrix to examine the short-term and long-term costs and benefits associated with drinking and not drinking.

You can use it whenever you're trying to figure out how to make the best choices for yourself. Anticipating the results of your behavior in advance offers you amazing control over your life. You'll be pleasantly surprised at how clear your options become when you're looking right at them. Chapter 9 addresses what to do with that special category of thoughts that drive behavior: sexual fantasies.

# Chapter Nine

# In Your Dreams

## Sexual Fantasy

"Sitting at her desk with her back very straight, she asks the young man very politely, the one who always comes into the library to check out bestsellers, asks him when it was he last got laid. He lets out a weird sound and she says, 'Shhh, this is a library.' She has her hair back and the glasses on but everyone has a librarian fantasy, and she is truly a babe beneath. 'I have a fantasy,' he says, 'of a librarian'" (Bender 1998).

Your sexual fantasies may have a different tone, subject matter, and scenario, but let's be honest, you have them. Sexual fantasy is one of the few remaining topics in Western society that people seldom discuss. Politics, religion, and actual sexual practices are wide-open for conversation in many circles, but sexual fantasy remains a fairly closed subject. Couples that pride themselves on their sexual lives may never whisper their fantasies between the sheets. People often avoid discussing them in treatment. Why?

### Desire

Fantasizing is often equated with dreaming, which can be thought of in two ways: either as losing oneself in a misty state outside of reality, or as a wish for something. We think that sexual fantasizing has to do with a wish for something. To discuss a sexual fantasy is somehow to admit that one has an unfulfilled sexual wish, and there can be some shame associated with having that type of longing.

Often, people avoid telling their partners they are not satisfied or that they desire something else sexually. Sometimes, they don't even like to admit it to themselves. They try to banish their fantasies from their thoughts. Forget about them. Get rid of them. At other times, they feed their fantasies, and then get lost in them.

**Getting rid of sexual fantasies isn't possible.**

It is very unlikely that you will be able to rid yourself of sexual fantasies, and even if you could do that, it would probably not be very helpful.

You may be surprised to hear that getting rid of your sexual fantasies isn't really possible. You probably thought you would have to endure a campaign to learn how to erase your sexual thoughts. Well, if erasure were possible, it just might work. But until the mind eraser is invented, you have to settle for the next-best treatment. What's that, you ask? Not what you expect. We challenge you to do *nothing* with your fantasies. This is not a joke. The best thing to do with sexual fantasies is exactly nothing.

## The Persistence of Thoughts

To explain the meaning of our statement, let's try a little experiment. We're going to tell you *not* to think of something and you're going to have to work really hard to do that. Are you ready? Don't think of pizza. Not even for a second. Don't think about the tangy sauce, the crispy crust, and cheese dripping over the edges. Don't think of the steam rising off of the top or how it smells when it's sitting in front of you. Don't think about the toppings you like to eat on it, or washing it down with a cold beer or soda. Now, put the book down for five minutes and try not to think about pizza.

How did you do? Did you do what we asked? You didn't? Well, why not? Didn't you try hard enough? All you had to do was not think about pizza. You could think about anything else in the world and you were still thinking about pizza? How could that be? Truthfully, this is a trick exercise. We know from psychological research that when you tell someone not to think about something, often it's all he or she can think about. Dr. Wegner and his colleagues have shown this effect repeatedly (1987; 1991). When they tell people not to think about a white bear, it's all they can think about. To top it all off, if the forbidden thought is about food, you can just throw in the towel. Mouths start watering, and people can imagine the taste and smell of the food almost as if it was in the room. So, you didn't have a chance.

It was important for you to do this exercise so you would experience a very important point for yourself. When you tell yourself not to think about something, you will think about it, sometimes even more than you would have done if you had not told yourself not to think about it. This may sound crazy, but it's true. What does that mean for sexual fantasies? It means that actively trying to make yourself not think sexual thoughts is most likely not going to work, and may in some cases cause fantasies to come up more often and with greater strength and staying power than previously.

**The first sexual fantasy mistake you can make is trying not to think of them.** If you've ever tried to control a craving, you know what we're talking about. If you were ever on a diet, think about how that was. Trying not to think about your favorite food was murder, remember? Recall how obsessed you became with ice cream, chips, or chocolate? Their allure was probably much greater than it was before you started the diet. That's the strange result of trying not to think about something. Sometimes the thoughts become stronger than they were when you began.

*Do nothing with your sexual fantasies.*

So, you have sexual fantasies; and probably many of them are related to whatever you do when you lose sexual self-control. Let them be.

As noted, people often try to get rid of their sexual fantasies or pretend they don't have them. That's the wrong way to go. Trying not to think about them may give them more energy. Also, some people go to the opposite extreme, which is to feed their fantasies. That is also a bad idea.

## Fueling Fantasy

As if having sexual fantasies doesn't provide enough excitement, sometimes people feed their fantasies. By "feeding" we mean making them longer, more detailed, and stronger than they started out. Sometimes people construct their fantasies to make them more arousing, working toward some kind of "perfection."

**The second sexual fantasy mistake is to build the original fantasy into something more elaborate.** For example, you might change the scenario, add more attractive sex partners in your preferred age range to your script, then have these sex partners madly attracted to you; then you get exactly the kind of sex you like, when you want it, and you end up feeling completely satisfied and content. Sometimes a fantasy is built on aspects of a real experience. Does this sound familiar? You add fuel to the fantasy to make it hotter. You want it to be just like a good book or movie, a story that's hard to put down. It can take over your life for a little while. You check out of reality and check into your daydream.

### Exercise: Describe Two Common Sexual Fantasy Mistakes

Two common sexual fantasy mistakes that lead to out-of-control behavior are

1. _____

2. _____

Another problem that arises when you add fuel to your fantasy is that it can cause the fantasy to get it stuck in your mind. You may become obsessed with it and be unable to free yourself from those sexual thoughts. These kinds of fantasies can interfere with your ability to function in everyday life. They also can make it impossible for you to lead a happy sexual life with normal people and in ordinary situations. There are no perfect people or conditions. We all have our flaws. If you start holding real-life situations up to the standards of your fantasies, there is no way they can measure up.

*Real-life sex often pales in comparison to sexual fantasies.*

So, you face constant disappointment and unmet expectations. We think that's one reason why some people with sexual self-control problems often end up living in fantasy worlds, barely noticing reality. They've shut themselves out of the real world by their need for the perfection of their fantasies.

## Case Example: Ang

Ang started off using porn pretty innocently. He told himself he was just satisfying his curiosity when he bought his first porn magazine. He thought his interest would be satisfied, and that would be it. But one magazine turned into a hidden collection of porn and hours and days of lost time. He became increasingly critical of his wife's appearance and their sex life. The women in his magazines loved sex and wanted it all the time. They were always beautiful, always dressed in lingerie, and always ready to try something new. He couldn't understand why his wife wasn't like that even some of the time.

Ang expected his wife to live up to the sex video he had created in his mind, the one where the women have nothing else to do but please men sexually. He changed the faces, the bodies, the places, and the activities into whatever he was in the mood for. He never considered the possibility that his fantasies might not be realistic, even for the women in the pictures. He was headed for a divorce and blamed his wife for not measuring up to his fantasy.

So, this is worth repeating just to be absolutely clear: Having sexual fantasies is normal. It's a part of life. Replacing your reality with fantasies is not normal. It's harmful to you and to those around you.

*Having sexual fantasies is healthy; letting them take over your life is not.*

It may be true that your life isn't going the way you would like it to, and it feels good to escape. It may seem as if fantasy is all you've got right now. Everyone escapes from reality from time to time. It becomes a problem when the fantasies get more of your attention than your life does, and when you start measuring your life by your daydreams. You can't very well change the way your life is going if you're floating in a daydream all the time. It's difficult even to become motivated to make your life better if you're constantly comparing it in a negative way with your fantasies. That's a 100 percent sure way to never have the life you want: Just ignore your life, and attend to your fantasies.

# Safe Fantasy

Now, let's talk about sexual fantasy as a substitution. If it's not something you depend on or something that takes over all of your time and energy, sexual fantasy can serve as a temporary substitution for sexual activities that are not available to you in reality. For example, let's imagine that you're someone who gets really excited by the thought of having sex with more than one person at a time. In reality, you don't want to have sex with more than one partner because you are worried about AIDS. So, every once in a while you have this fantasy. It starts up your arousal, and you have great sex with your partner. This is not a problem. It's a passing fancy.

## *Fantasy and Reality*

When your fantasizing becomes obsessive thinking or planning, then it has become a problem. Obsessive thinking takes place when you can't stop thinking about a fantasy. You can't get it out of your mind. Remember, when fantasy takes the place of reality, it's too much, and it's unhealthy. Here, "planning" means that instead of having the fantasy occasionally, you begin to figure out—to plan—how you can make it, or something like it, happen. This is when fantasy crosses the line. A fantasy is a fantasy precisely because there are no downsides to it. There are no costs involved. Real life does not work that way. When fantasizing turns to planning, costs must be involved in the plot as well. It is possible that the costs could be low.

> *When fantasizing turns to obsessing or planning, it's too much.*

For example, suppose that you want to try oral sex with your new girlfriend for the first time. You've been imagining it for weeks. You bring condoms and at the right moment, you suggest it. Of course there's some risk of the condom breaking, of her saying no, of embarrassment, and so on, but the costs are low. You would have considered the costs and benefits and the benefits would have won out. This would be good planning and decision making.

Now, think about your most frequent sexual fantasy for a few minutes, and after you've got it going, answer the question in the exercise below.

### Exercise: Figuring Out the Costs of Your Fantasy

What are the real costs that would be associated with living out your fantasy?

1. _____

2. _____

3. _____

4. _____

Now, imagine that your fantasy involves having sex with someone who is underage. Planning this kind of fantasy must include a consideration of the costs. Everyone knows about the potential damage that is done to young people who have sex with adults, even if they don't protest in the moment. Along with mental health problems, you have to consider that your underage sex partner could have sexual problems later in life, develop alcoholism or drug abuse, or become involved in prostitution. You could go to prison or lose your job, family, reputation, ability to work, and so on. In this instance, the fantasy doesn't come close to matching what the reality could cost. When fantasizing turns to planning, costs must be examined. And, typically, what you're going to find in most cases is that the reality does not support the fantasy.

*Real-world costs pop the fantasy bubble.*

Reality is constrained in ways that imagination is not. That's why most fantasies are best kept in the fantasy world. Keeping your fantasies in the dream world where they belong is a good idea unless the costs that go with acting them out are very low (and you must be realistic about evaluating the costs). At the same time, we are also saying that you should not spend too much of your life on fantasies. Spending your days lost in your thoughts really diminishes life. What's the point of living if you aren't involved in the world? Parts III, IV, and V of this book will teach you how to build the kind of life you've always wanted. You can create a rich and varies life that puts your fantasies to shame.

# Part Three

# How Can You Change If
# You Feel So Bad?

# Chapter Ten

# Nothing More Than Feelings

What would you do if you found out you had a brain tumor and had only one more month to live? Would you get a second opinion? Cry? Jump off the nearest bridge? Get drunk? Travel? Throw a party? What would you do if your life were about to end painfully? Would you endure the pain to make time to create a few more memories, or would you try to avoid the pain as soon as possible? Would you beg for morphine? Would you hide yourself away, rarely to be seen? How would you cope with that kind of situation?

## Pain Avoidance

Along with the many privileges of living in wealthy societies, it seems that Westerners have also developed an intolerance for pain. It's as though it's been decided that suffering is a problem that can always be fixed with good old-fashioned ingenuity. So, there are numerous solutions for the problem of pain. Countless options have been developed to reduce physical pain. Drug companies are among the richest businesses in the world. Emotional pain is a bit more challenging a problem, but we have spiritual practices, entertainment, consumerism, drugs, therapy, and sex to counter it. The days of "no pain, no gain" are long past.

Western society has evolved into a culture of pain avoidance. The message broadcast day and night on TV and other media is that feeling bad is not normal. It states that feeling happy is expected of everyone all of the time. The message implies that if you aren't happy, something must be wrong with you, and you need to fix it. As a result of this widespread idea, people work hard to feel happy. They buy bigger TV sets, work out at home and in gyms, drink alcohol at home and in bars, swallow aspirins and other painkillers, and talk with friends to feel good.

## Exercise: How Do You Avoid Feeling Bad?

In the space provided below, list some of the ways that you typically use to avoid feeling bad.

_____

_____

_____

_____

# Emotional Control: The Myth

There's a big problem with any of these avoidance strategies. That problem can be summed up with this sentence: People cannot completely control how they feel, at least not for very long. Here is an example. Suppose you're out on the road in your new car. You're going through an intersection and suddenly, from out of nowhere, your car is struck by another vehicle. You're not hurt, but how do you feel? Pretty angry, no doubt. In the aftermath of the accident you discover that the driver of the other car is a student who was behind the wheel for the first time. You probably won't feel any less angry. Maybe you would be less angry with the driver, but you're still likely to be extremely irritated. You might not scream at the driver, but your angry feelings would still be there.

*Controlling feelings is difficult.*

Feelings just don't make sense. They sometimes show up even when logic tells you they shouldn't. It's true that it's possible to reason your way through them and to lessen their intensity. You are unlikely to attack the driver of the other car since a student driver couldn't have been expected to drive well, but the accident triggered your anger and you may stay angry for a while.

If something has made you sad and someone tells you not to feel sad about it, can you do that? Honestly, is it possible to not feel sad anymore? You might be able to distract yourself from it or ignore it for a while. You might even be able to turn your sadness into anger or some other emotion, but to actually get rid of it so that it never returns? That's not likely. That's a task humans are not very good at doing.

What about the opposite, that is, can you make yourself feel something on purpose? Can you do it? You can recall feelings easily. For instance, you can bring up feelings that are associated with a romantic song. But can you create feelings out of thin air? For example, if we offered you $100 to feel sad about someone killing a fly, could you do it? The feeling would have to be real. Could you pump up some real feeling for that fly? Probably you could think of a time in the past when you were sad and you could use your memories of that experience. You might be able to conjure up some sadness, but could you make yourself feel truly sad about the fly's demise? It's not likely.

Feelings are triggered by

- Situations

- Thoughts

- Other feelings

- Physical sensations

It is possible to control feelings or to hide them, but, typically, they surface and then fade away before we even are aware of them. So, we're always lagging behind, a bit surprised when it's time to cope with how we feel. You may be thinking, what does any of this have to do with your sexual self-control problem? Well, it turns out that how you feel has a lot to do with sexual self-control.

*Controlled feelings may come back later.*

Many people spend a lot of time and energy trying to control how they feel. They try to distract themselves from what they feel, get rid of it, or replace it with some forced happiness. The crazy part of this is that the feelings people don't want to feel don't simply go away. Instead, they just sort of hide out for a while, only to pop up at other, often inconvenient, times, according to research done by Wegner and Zanakos (1994) and Wenzlaff, Wegner, and Klein (1991). Allowing themselves to lose sexual control is one way that many people try to deal with their feelings. They try to manage their emotions with sex.

### Exercise: Fill in the Blank

Controlled feelings commonly _____ again.

## Unwanted Feelings

How many times have you gone out looking for sexual satisfaction when you felt lonely, rejected, sad, angry, disrespected, frustrated, anxious, depressed, scared, unloved, or hurt? The feeling might have come up just before you took sexual action, or it could have been hanging around off and on for hours or days. It's very likely that when you got into some out-of-control sexual situations they were related to feeling bad. Just as some people use drugs, smoking, overeating, overwork, or hobbies to feel better, you use sex and sex-related activities to make yourself feel better.

**Using sex to feel better is common.**

You may even find that you use more than one of these coping strategies. That's normal. These are ways that people use to try to manage life's difficulties. Unfortunately, these strategies are like life preservers with no air in them. They may look as if they can save you, but in reality, if you hold onto one, you'll sink faster.

If having outrageous sex could make you feel better or create a better life for you, don't you think it would have happened by now? You've been telling yourself that your problem is that you haven't had enough sex or you haven't yet experienced the exactly right sexual high. These are lies, self-deceptions that allow you to keep your sex-related activities going strong. Your problem is not whether you've had enough sex, partners, or variety. The problem is that sex, despite its lure and the promises it offers, cannot make you feel better, not in any real or lasting sense.

**Sex cannot fix hurt feelings.**

It's true that for a short time you may forget about what else is going on in your life. You may be distracted from whatever you are feeling. And because of the false promise of sex, you keep going back for more. You keep thinking that someday sex is going to deliver the solution to all of your problems if you just get it right. These are all lies. As everyone knows, the problems are right there waiting for you when you becme vertical again. The problem is not that you've been doing it wrong; the problem is that your entire approach *cannot* be successful. Sex cannot permanently change your feelings.

## Exercise: What Kind of Fix Is Sex?

**Is sex a short-term fix?** Yes or No

**Or is it a long-term solution?** Yes or No

Circle the correct answer. Then, in the space provided below, write out three reasons for choosing the answer you did.

1. _____

2. _____

3. _____

Where does this leave you? It's been made clear that you can't change your feelings. They just happen. But, you can make a couple of constructive moves when they come up. The first rule sounds as if it is easy. In fact, it sounds simpler than it is.

**The first and only rule is this: Do nothing with your feelings.** Now, for someone like you—someone who's been trying to control feelings with sex—following this rule isn't going to be natural or easy, but it is possible to do it.

*Do nothing with your feelings and they will change.*

Feelings, if you don't try to get rid of them, come and go rather quickly and easily. Typically, they last for a few minutes and are then replaced by new feelings. They come and go, each following the other. This system is tripped up when silly ideas arise about controlling feelings or hanging onto them. When people try to control their emotions, the feelings don't get the chance to dissolve as they normally would. Instead, they keep coming back. Bad feelings are like fruitcakes. Nobody likes them, but every so often they show up, to your dismay. You can't purposefully get rid of them in any reliable way. On the other hand, when people choose to wallow in their feelings for some time, their emotions tend to become stronger than they were ever meant to be and they last long past their natural "expiration date."

The bottom line is that trying to control feelings doesn't work very well. Instead, you've got to let them pass. Notice them. Practice calling them by their names. For instance, telling yourself what you are feeling in the moment (irritated or worried, for example) is a great habit to develop. Practice naming your feelings to yourself as you would practice learning any new skill. If you do that, then the feeling doesn't seem to be in control. There's no mystery to it. It's just something that is there. And it will pass. You don't have to do anything about it, it will pass.

## Exercise: What Are You Feeling Now?

Take a moment to identify how you are feeling right now. Then write down what you are feeling in the space provided below. Practice identifying your feelings every day.

I am feeling  _____

You might also want to reassure yourself that you are going to make it through the feeling without dying. This may sound funny, but it may apply to you. You may feel an emotion you don't like and you may think that if you go on feeling it without doing something sexual to stop it, then you're going to die because the feeling is too strong to tolerate. Every time this happens, your job is to tolerate the unwanted feeling and do something that is not on your sexual chain. For example,

*Being able to tolerate feeling bad leads to sexual self-control.*

you could read a magazine or you could exercise. You'll be surprised how quickly the unwanted feeling will pass. And, you will not have done anything to make your situation worse.

*Instant happiness is a myth.*

Keep in mind the fact that this approach won't make you instantly happy. Feeling happy is not the point. The point is that you can feel your feelings without being manipulated by them. Greater emotional stability is a firm foundation for great things to happen in your life. Learning to let your feelings come and go naturally is just one step toward making your life more livable and meaningful.

Sometimes tolerating unwanted emotions will be difficult, because sometimes the hand that life deals you is full of hardships. The important thing to remember is that you can handle any of your feelings that come up. You have a choice about whether or not to act out sexually and create more suffering. It is the same for positive feelings, the ones you'd like to last for a while. Leave them alone. Like any other feeling, positive feelings come and go. Trying to intensify them to make them last so that you won't have to feel anything bad is pointless.

Trying to manipulate your feelings

- Takes a lot of energy

- Doesn't work

- Steals energy and attention away from the rest of your life

If you're working to stay happy, it's hard to create the kind of life you want at the same time.

## Sexual Feelings

Now we have some special advice for what to do with your sexual feelings. What do you do when you're feeling horny, excited, hot, aroused, and amorous? Nothing. That's right. Absolutely nothing. You're probably protesting now. Hopefully, you've picked the book up off the floor so that we can continue.

Frequently, people with sexual self-control problems have a false belief that comes up whenever we talk about feeling sexually aroused. They believe that they *have* to do something about it no matter what. This is a lie that keeps their sexual behavior going and keeps them (and you!) in trouble. People feel aroused all the time and don't act on the feeling. You wouldn't think this is so based on television, films, and the tabloids, but it's true. Happily married people are sometimes attracted to other people, but they manage not to have affairs. Many priests and nuns feel sexual attractions, but they honor their celibacy vows for their entire lives. Some young people wait until they are

*You don't have to act on your sexual feelings.*

married to have sex. These people are not supercontrollers, neither are they robots. They are ordinary people who have sexual feelings who've made their choices about sex. You can make similar choices about your problematic sexual behaviors.

Again, not acting out sexually involves noticing and tolerating your arousal. And, of course, this doesn't mean that you will never be sexually satisfied again.

In part V of this book, we discuss how to create a satisfying and safe sex life. A large part of being in control of your sexuality is having a satisfying sex life that is not harmful to you or anyone else. Learning to tolerate arousal without being sexual is a gift you can give to yourself. You're strengthening your ability to tolerate discomfort. You're dealing with a little discomfort now to avoid a lot of discomfort later on. With your newly found tolerance, you also gain new freedom and inner strength. You don't have to be controlled by your feelings. You can tolerate them and control your behavior and, ultimately, your life.

*Noticing and tolerating your sexual arousal leads to sexual self-control.*

## Feeling and Doing

People often ask how they can change when they feel so bad. They have the false notion that they have to feel okay in order to do something different with their lives. They think that to act differently they have to "feel like it." But this is just one more false belief that keeps them living their old lives. Feeling has nothing to do with doing.

If you wait for your feelings to fall in line with what you'd like to do with your life, you may as well wait for the sky to fall. It's not going to happen. Do you think Michael Jordan felt like playing basketball every day? It's been reported that he played when he had life problems, injuries, and illnesses. And he played spectacularly. New mothers don't usually feel like leaving their babies with other caretakers and returning to work, but they do. Why? They need the income or they value their careers, and they do what they need to do. Firefighters, police, and paramedics work day and night, sometimes for days, to save the victims of terrible tragedies. Do they feel like doing what they do? It's doubtful. They do it because it is in line with what they want for their lives. You can do the same. If there was ever a time for you to rise to the occasion and do what needs to be done, it is now. No more excuses. Make your changes, no matter how you feel.

*Doing cannot depend on feeling.*

# Chapter Eleven

# You're Good Enough, You're Smart Enough, and People Like You

Who can forget actress Sally Field's speech at the Oscar awards when in a flood of emotion she blurted out, "You like me, you really like me!" It was an admission of vulnerability to the opinions of others that few people make, but most experience on a regular basis. We care about what other people think about us. From that first note in grade school that said, "I like you. If you like me, check this box," to dates and opinion polls, we've cared about what people think about us.

## Opinion Sensitivity

Beyond our day-to-day concerns, we also have a kind of "radar" for negative thoughts about ourselves. Even when others are not talking or thinking about us, we think they are. Whispers, glances, and laughs make us worry. We'd all like to be free from caring about what others think of us, and sometimes we even manage to escape for a while. We tell ourselves we don't care. We rebel, and then we secretly worry about what other people think about the fact that we don't care anymore and are acting like rebels.

## People Pleasing

It's difficult to get away from the power of public opinion, but in order to make lasting life changes, we must escape it because it robs us of our ability to be comfortable with who we are. How does that work?

*By focusing on pleasing others, we may lose ourselves.*

Public opinion ruins us in several ways. First, when we care about others' opinions of us, we may act in ways we think will please them. We may become chameleons, changing our colors to match the scenery. Or sometimes we won't act in line with our own goals and beliefs because we choose to make other people more important than ourselves. We pursue *their* goals and values because we are trying to win their approval. What is important to us disappears. Another byproduct of people pleasing is that if everyone doesn't like or accept us, we experience unpleasant feelings such as loneliness, anxiety, sadness, anger, and frustration. Our lives may become filled with emotions that, while not totally disabling us, make it fairly difficult to continue at a normal pace.

### Exercise: Negative Outcomes of People Pleasing

In the space provided below, list some of the negative outcomes you've experienced from trying to please other people.

_____

_____

_____

_____

## The Self-Fulfilling Prophecy

Beyond spending valuable time trying to please others, we may take others' opinions about us as truth. We may begin to believe what others think about us, and from that we may form a negative view of who we are. Even worse, we can act as if what others think and say about us is true. That is called a "self-fulfilling prophecy." You end up doing what others expect of you, not because it was in your plans, but because it was expected to happen.

And finally, when we care too much about what other people think of us, we often try to win them over with false behavior. We don't act like ourselves; we stop being genuine. This can leave us with even more reason to feel ashamed and inferior. Plus, when we are being fake, it is detectable. What we do or say may feel false to the very people we're trying to please. That's when people pleasing really backfires. There you are, working hard to please others, and they don't like you because they think you are a big phony. It all boils down to the fact that if we are not being who we really are in our relationships, we are not being true to our values and goals.

Although it's true that being liked is helpful in life, being liked at all costs is not. Dr. O'Donohue likes to use the example of Hitler. If Hitler were alive today, would you really want him to like you? Some of us want everyone to like us all of the time, but that's not realistic. If you are living in line with what you care about, you are going to rub someone else the wrong way. It's the natural result of living by your principles. Somebody isn't going to agree with you and he or she may not even like you. We like to call it the Frank Sinatra effect. The song he is most famous for is "My Way." What did he do? He drove other people crazy while living life *his* way.

*Meaningful goals are lost in people pleasing.*

It turns out that when we focus on what people think of us, we are focused on exactly the wrong thing. When we spend our limited energy managing what others think of us, we lose energy we could be spending on working toward our goals in a responsible way. The natural result of focusing on our values and goals is that the people who are right for us will like us, and the others won't matter. Being popular is not the same as being productive.

## Goals and Self-Acceptance

Go back to chapter 4 and review all of your lists of goals. Take some time out from reading right now so that you can recall what is important to you. Typically, your goals will fall into two categories. The first category is to have good relationships with others, and the second is to make a meaningful life. Of course, your goals were more specific. For example, you might have said you wanted to spend time with your children every day, or to work more diligently so that you could enjoy your job. These goals are the compass for your life. They lead the way for you. How other people feel about you is not a compass, it's the wind. How someone feels about you can be as temperamental as a storm. Trying to control the wind is a pretty difficult job. Just ask Mother Nature.

Some of your goals may have to do with people. You may be wondering how those goals relate to trying to impress people. Well, let's break it down. If you value building relationships with people, the whole idea is that they must be *real* relationships. They aren't based on some fake version of yourself. If you scam someone into becoming your friend, either you're going to have to keep pretending for a very long time, or the friend is going to realize that you are not who you made yourself out to be. Either way, you end up with a disappointing relationship. In order to create real, meaningful relationships you have to be yourself.

That does not mean that everyone you want to be in a relationship with will want to be in a relationship with you, even if you are being yourself. If they know the real you and that doesn't suit them, it's not a relationship that was written in the stars. There are people who will appreciate you for who you are. They will appreciate your goals and your way of being. They will support the person you are trying to become and what you are trying to do with your life. Relationships don't get much better than that.

*Be yourself.*

Now that you are in touch with your goals again, ask yourself why you've been working to earn someone else's approval. Is it because you think he or she doesn't like you? Do you think you are less than that person is? Do you think you need that person's approval to get ahead? What's the reason? Think of some examples in your life right now.

Once, Dr. Penix Sbraga was talking with one of the most influential psychologists in America. He told her that after all of his successes and twenty-five years in psychology, he still feels the urge to please people, especially people in powerful positions. People pleasing affects most of us, no matter how successful we become. The first step toward breaking this bad habit is to identify your goals, which you've already done. What's important in your life is the base from which you can operate.

## Self-Acceptance

The next step is to transfer your need for acceptance from outside to inside. Right now, you may look for acceptance from other people and try to influence and control their acceptance of you. If that is so, you're fighting a losing battle. Acceptance has to come from within. What does that mean? It means that how you view yourself must be separated and untangled from how others see you. Your view of yourself has to be based on two things: who you are and what your goals and values are.

Who you are is someone who is worth something no matter what you do or have done. You are worthy of living just because you exist, not for any other reason. Many people operate under the assumption that they must be productive and esteemed members of society to be of value. One of our clients made a particularly strong statement in this regard. She told Dr. Penix Sbraga that if she were ever in an accident and became disabled, she would kill herself because she would no longer be of any use to her family. It took her a long time to understand that her kids would still love and need her, even if she couldn't do anything for them.

*You are valuable.*

Are those who don't make visible contributions to society valuable? Of course they are. And your life is valuable too.

You may have tried to discount your life, but it is valuable anyway. Often, we judge ourselves by how much we measure up to other people and what they are doing in the world. This is not a fair standard to measure yourself by. You came into this world with a unique makeup, grew up with a unique set of influences and resources, and you have done what you could with whatever you had, up to this point. Now, because you are reading this book, you have new information at your disposal. You can do more and make changes with more resources. Again, this is not about measuring up in the eyes of others. We don't care if you win the Nobel Peace Prize. This is about doing what you were made to do. Doing what is inside of you. You were made for more than chasing sex.

### Exercise: Know Yourself as a Valuable Person

Now, take a few minutes to recognize yourself as a valuable person. If you have any difficulty, think of how you were when you were a small child who had not gotten into any trouble yet. You are still the same person. Your body has changed, but at the core, you are the same. Then, after you've thought about this for a while, write down three reasons why you are a valuable person.

1. _____

2. _____

3. _____

Taking control of your sex life is a huge step toward feeling good about yourself. Putting the rest of your life into balance and building it around what is important to you is next. Self-acceptance, self-confidence, and good feelings will flow naturally from living your life focused on what is important to you.

## Imperfection and Self-Correction

*Be imperfect, but self-correcting.*

When you start getting down on yourself, as most people do regularly, have a little self-talk. Ask yourself, why you can't screw up occasionally. Everyone else does from time to time. Sometimes we do something with the best of intentions, put our hearts into it, and it still doesn't work out the way we would like it to. People make mistakes. That's the name of the game. Nobody's perfect. Why can't we admit that to ourselves and move on? The point is to be self-correcting and not look to others for their approval.

If you're working within your set of values and you make a mistake, just notice it, correct the problem, and move on. There's no need to get down on yourself. How is that useful? You just feel worse, and feeling bad about yourself makes it harder to get back on your feet and do what you need to do. Putting yourself down doesn't make you a better or more productive person.

Even if you are living a life that is completely in line with what you care about, you will sometimes feel down about yourself. You will think negative thoughts about yourself and your abilities. Sometimes these internal reactions come up no matter what we do. We've learned to think and feel in specific ways, and old habits die hard.

## Exercise: Dealing with Negative Self-Thoughts

1. When these reactions come up, just notice them for what they are—shadows from the past that keep hanging around.

2. Then use the new skills you learned in chapter 6 about how to recognize when your thoughts are distorted.

*Thinking negative thoughts about yourself doesn't make them true.*

3. When you've done that, use the skills you practiced in chapter 10 to better tolerate your thoughts and feelings.

4. Remember, feeling bad won't kill you. It won't even injure you. You just have to get through it without doing anything reckless and continue working toward your goals.

## Exercise: Match the Term with Its Description

Match the following terms with their correct descriptions below. Draw a line from the term to its description. The answers appear upside down under the exercise.

1. acceptance
2. people pleasing
3. self-fulfilling prophecy
4. tolerance
5. self-correcting

a. taking things as they are
b. doing what was expected of you
c. trying to make others happy
d. learning from mistakes and changing
e. putting up with something

1a; 2c; 3b; 4e; 5d

## *Living Life on Your Own Terms*

Question: What can you do if someone clearly doesn't like you?

Answer: Figure out your goals for both the situation and the relationship. If the relationship is important to you in some way, you may need to make a plan for how to meet your goals in spite of that person not liking you. Remember, it is not the point to please the other person. The point is to live in line with what is important to you.

For example, suppose you start dating a woman who has a teenage daughter who can't stand you. You care about your relationships with both the mother and the daughter. But your move is not to try to win the girl over. The idea is to behave in accord with your caring about both of them. So, you might act in a warm, friendly way to her, tolerate her dislike of you without retaliating, and refuse to speak badly about her. A second benefit of acting this way might be that she might grow to like you. But that is not the goal. The point is to act in line with your goal of being a caring person with the people in your life.

Maybe the teenager has some valid reasons for not liking you. If you are working at creating a valued relationship, you can listen to her point of view without feeling defensive. You can evaluate her point of view based on what is important to you, not on trying to seem like a good boy-friend or father figure. Perhaps there are things you can change about your behavior with her or her mother that you simply didn't see before she let you know about them. If that happens, the teenager will have helped you out by increasing your understanding. Your reaction to the situation either can increase the divide between you, or it can provide an opportunity for both of you to grow.

*Use your goals as your guide.*

On the other hand, if the problematic relationship doesn't fit into your goals and values in any way, why waste energy on it? Don't be drawn into drama. Accept that the person does not like you and move on.

We offer one final word on acting like a screwup just because it is expected of you. This is not useful for anyone. It's just one more way of looking to other people to tell you how you should be, feel, think, and act. It pulls you way off target and puts you at ground zero when it comes to living a meaningful life. Don't do it. Situations and people will come and go, thoughts and feelings will come and go, but you get to decide who and what is important to you and what to do about it. Never let anyone else make your life-defining decisions for you.

*Don't let others live your life for you.*

# Chapter Twelve

# Who's Hurting Here?

Have you ever heard the story about the businessman who went to Las Vegas, picked up a woman in a bar, and woke up the next day in an ice-filled bathtub with a missing kidney and a note to call 911? What about the one where Neiman Marcus said it would charge a woman "two fifty" for a cookie recipe, and then charged her credit card $250, and she, for revenge, sent the secret recipe over the Internet to as many people as possible? Or perhaps you've heard the one about a male celebrity who went to the emergency room to have a gerbil surgically removed from his rectum?

If you live in the United States, you have undoubtedly heard one or all of these stories at one time or another. They are often called "urban legends." These are new myths passed by word of mouth from person to person as truths. Typically, the person telling the story heard it from a friend, who heard it from a friend, and so on down the line. The friend connection makes the story believable and the tale grows stronger with each retelling.

People are intrigued by outrageous stories that could be true. If they stand to gain something if the story is true, even better. For example, among college students, the myth of receiving a perfect grade point average from the authorities if a roommate has committed suicide is treated as if it were the gospel truth. If we want to believe in something, we are easily convinced of the accuracy of that thing. We believe more quickly and firmly in beliefs that we find attractive. You've wanted to believe that you haven't harmed anyone with your sexual misbehavior. You've wanted to minimize the ripple effect your loss of control has had on other people.

*Stories about out-of-control sexual behavior make it seem harmless.*

# Sexual Side-Effects

To do the work in this chapter, you must be painfully honest with yourself and face the fact that you've probably spun some untruthful stories about how you haven't hurt anyone. You've held these tales close to your heart for a long time. Maybe you've told them to other people, but it's very likely that you've put yourself to sleep with them a few times. Now it's time to examine the stories you tell yourself about the people you come into contact with and be truthful about what your effect on these people has been.

We're not interested in punishing you. Neither do we want to make you feel bad about your sexual actions. We are not the courts or your parents. We are interested in helping you learn to see your life clearly, with a magnifying glass if necessary, so you can change those behaviors that, on closer inspection, have been harmful to others. It is also important to understand that you are a victim of your own behavior as well.

Throughout this book we've discussed the fact that your feelings have a lot to do with your loss of self-control. You suffer because of what you do sexually. Feeling blue, down, angry, rejected, lonely, frustrated, guilty, irritated, anxious, hurt, and so forth, are regular occurrences for you. We know you are pained by your actions. So, this chapter offers you a chance to get in touch with the people who are on the receiving end of your actions.

*You hurt yourself as well as others when you engage in out-of-control sex.*

You may be saying to yourself that you haven't hurt anyone with your sexual behavior. Maybe you've only exposed yourself, bought porn, or hung out at topless clubs. Or perhaps you never make physical contact with anyone sexually. For you, it's the Internet, phone sex, and pay-per-view. If you're letting yourself off the hook because these are your practices, and you've never actually sexually assaulted anyone, please keep an open mind. People are harmed by your sexual behavior in ways you may have never even thought about. There is a trickle-down effect that reaches farther than you've imagined. Your sexual behavior has created victims if

1. You spend any money on your sexual habits except for condoms or birth control methods

2. You view pornography

3. You pay for sex legally or illegally

4. You don't take no for an answer in sexual situations

5. You make commitments to your family, friends, or boss that you don't honor because of your sexual activities

6. You don't take care of yourself

7. You keep sexual secrets

8. You ask other people to keep your sexual secrets

9. You make sexual satisfaction your first priority

10. You mistreat your sexual partner(s)

*There are hidden victims of lost sexual self-control.*

You might ask, "How, am I harming anyone?" If you spend money on your sexual habits, that cash is not available for other purchases. Perhaps you aren't paying your bills and someone else pays them for you. Maybe the money you spend on sex means your kids don't have new school clothes. Maybe you can't afford to buy even a modest anniversary present for your parents, and you know a gift from you would mean a lot to them. Perhaps you've infected someone you care about with a sexually transmitted disease. Maybe you spend all of your time on the telephone or computer or in front of the TV instead of making time for friends or family members.

## Exercise: How You Hurt Loved Ones with Your Sexual Behavior

In the space provided below, list five of the ways you hurt family members or friends with your sexual behavior.

1. _____

_____

2. _____

_____

3. _____

_____

4. _____

_____

5. _____

_____

Spending your money on sex supports the sex industry. Do you remember the statistics that appeared in chapter 2? The sex industry may be the largest money empire in the world. Your contributions are making it even richer and more powerful. You are adding money to the purse that pays for women and children to be abducted from their homes so they can be employed as sexual slaves in the international sex industry. You are making prostitutes and strippers out of people who could and would do something else for a living if they had a reasonable choice. You are paying people to risk their health so you can get some sexual kicks.

Maybe you fantasize about working in the porn industry. Getting paid to have sex sounds pretty good to you, right? The reality of the porn industry, however, looks nothing like your dream about working for it.

*When you lose control, you hurt your family and friends.*

Porn actors often get into the business because they are desperate for money and think they can't do anything else. They don't have the chance to find out what else they could do, because they have sex with strangers in front of a camera for a few bucks. Most of them do not become stars. They do not love sex. They do not get rich. They do not become legitimate Hollywood actors. Instead, they get AIDS. They get stuck in the sex business because no one else will hire them. They get depressed and suicidal to boot. Does that sound glamorous?

You may say to yourself that porn actors have a choice about whether to do porn or not. After all, they can always find work at McDonald's, right? Thinking like this is called "blaming the victim." It's your mind's way of getting you off the hook. The truth is that porn exists to satisfy your appetite for it. If you and your "compadres" no longer bought porn, there would be no porn actors and no negative consequences.

Along the same lines, you may think that prostitutes choose to hustle, right? It's their decision. Wrong. The majority of prostitutes are forced to have sex for money. You don't know what goes on behind the scenes. Working girls and gigolos are not sex-crazed people who want to sell their bodies for fun and games. They are people desperate to make ends meet or to keep someone from hurting them. Working the streets and escort services is dangerous. Your behavior is creating jobs that these people are forced to fill, and you are putting them in harm's way. People in the sex industry do their jobs not because they want to, but because they have to. Working mothers may have phone sex lines coming into their homes because they cannot afford day care. Their children listen to sexually explicit talk because people call for the service. What is the impact this kind of language has on young, developing minds?

*People associated with the sex industry are hurt by it.*

## Exercise: What Does "Blaming the Victim" Mean?

In the space provided, write your own definition of what "blaming the victim" means. If you can come up with something from your own life where you were at fault, but you blamed the person who was hurt by your actions, that would be very helpful for you.

Blaming the victim is _____

_____

_____

## Case Example: Sheila

Sheila was a prostitute who was treated by Dr. Penix Sbraga. She and her friends, other hookers, were struggling financially and in their personal lives. She hardly made enough money to pay her rent and take care of her son. In the course of her work, Sheila had been beaten and raped many times. That caused her to become very fearful of going out alone, and she carried a gun for her own protection. When she was turning tricks, she looked as if she loved every minute of it. She said she "painted a smile on her face." Her pride kept her from allowing her customers to see her misery. But at home with her son, she couldn't stop crying. She had not enjoyed sex for years and was unable to have a relationship with a man because she couldn't talk about her work and she couldn't have a normal sexual relationship. Despite her beauty and outgoing personality, Sheila believed she was "damaged goods," and that no man would ever want to live with her. Her son was ashamed of her and she had no friends outside of the sex industry. Do you still think that Sheila leads a glamorous life?

## Exercise: How You Hurt Strangers with Your Sexual Behavior

In the space provided, list five ways you hurt strangers with your sexual behavior. Remember, the major ways in which strangers are harmed by you are by-products of the various sex industries that you support.

1. _____

2. _____

3. _____

4. _____

5. _____

## Forced Sex

What about talking people into sex, just pushing them a little? What harm does that do? When people resist sex, *they don't want it*. Yes, you can overpower them with charm, persistence, or even a little force. But it's wrong and it's hurtful. You may harm someone physically if you try to force him or her to have sex with you. And emotional damage commonly results.

*Acquaintances are hurt by your out-of-control sexual behavior.*

When people are forced into having sex, it destroys their ability to trust. How can they ever trust anyone again? Can they handle being alone? Can they leave the house? Can they go on a date? When you override someone's free will you take away a fundamental part of who they are; the part that gets to decide what each person does with his or her own body. Some people might laugh nervously and go along with the sex after you've ignored their "No!" not because they changed their mind, but *because he or she is afraid of you*.

You might get a kick out of having that kind of power over someone, but look at all the damage you're doing. With that one act of overpowering someone for sex, it's likely that you are causing mental health problems, drug abuse, sexual problems, social problems, work problems, and health problems. You may never get arrested. You might not experience any negative consequences for forcing sex on someone. But the costs are there. You're just making someone else pay for your mistakes.

Maybe you don't force people to have sex with you. Maybe you lure acquaintances into having sex with the promise of a meaningful relationship with you. Maybe you lie to get what you what from them. Perhaps you have one-night stands, treating your partners well until you have an orgasm and then verbally abusing them afterward. In these situations, after you are through with them, the people you used and barely knew may find it more difficult to trust others. They may become fearful of sex or relationships. Or they may experience shame or self-hatred, all because of their sexual contact with you. These are examples of the harm your sexual behavior can cause acquaintances.

### Exercise: How You Hurt Acquaintances with Your Sexual Behavior

In the space provided below, list five ways you hurt acquaintances with your sexual behavior.

1. _____

2. _____

_____

3. _____

_____

4. _____

_____

5. _____

_____

## Disappointed People

People with sexual self-control problems typically let down their families, friends, and coworkers too. How many times have you promised to be somewhere and then missed the appointment because you were out pursuing sex? How many times have you refused to help out with something because it would cut into your sex time? How many times have you promised to give up your habit so you could have better relationships with the people who are closest to you, only to disappoint them again and again? You are slowly chipping away at your important relationships. Friends and relatives pick up the pieces time and time again. They are worse off because they are associated with you. Not because of who you are, but because of the sexual things you do.

*Associating with you has an ugly downside.*

### Case Example: Rachel and Michael

Take Rachel, for example. She was on top of the world when she started dating Michael. They met at work and immediately discovered that they shared common interests and hobbies. So, it was no surprise they were soon spending all of their days and nights together. They both enjoyed sex and worked to keep it creative and satisfying.

Despite their compatibility, however, Rachel felt that she couldn't really get close to Michael. There seemed to be a wall between them. He wouldn't talk about his past except superficially, and at times he was cold and distant without any apparent reason. She was confused because he said that he loved her and wanted a serious relationship, but he wasn't sharing himself with her. Rachel told herself that, with time, he would learn to trust her and his walls would come down.

About a year after they started dating, Rachel discovered the reason for Michael's distant behavior. They had been on a train trip together but the train was so crowded they had to sit in separate seats. About an hour into the trip, at a railway station, the conductor came to her and asked if she was with Michael. Assuming he was going to seat them together, she said, "Yes." He then told her to get her bags and get off the train with Michael. He said they would have to take the next train.

Rachel was outraged and she pleaded with him to tell her what was going on. She couldn't understand why he kept saying she should talk to Michael. While she was getting off the train, she saw a young woman looking at her with disgust. The woman pointed at Rachel and said to the person beside her, "She's with him." Rachel couldn't understand why anyone would look at her with such contempt.

When she met up with Michael on the platform, he refused to speak to her or even to look at her until they had arrived home. Rachel couldn't imagine what had happened. She was frightened and very confused. Were their tickets counterfeit? Had that woman who had looked at her with such disgust started a fight with Michael? What could it be?

When they arrived home, he told his story. He asked Rachel if she knew anything about *paraphilias,* which is a pattern of sexual behavior that involves unusual and socially unacceptable sexual practices. He then explained he had a problem that involved exposing himself to unsuspecting strangers and that he had masturbated in front of the woman sitting next to him on the train. He told Rachel that he had been in treatment for the problem before he met her, and he had thought he had it under control. His shame and misery were apparent because as he spoke, he trembled and sobbed.

Michael said that he'd been afraid Rachel would leave him if she knew about his problem and his past. He told her that he hadn't been able to trust that she would continue to care for him, so he was never able to be truly intimate with her. He'd always held a part of himself back from her in case she found out.

Rachel felt as if she was riding an emotional roller coaster. One strong emotion after another flooded her body. She had never experienced the kind of humiliation she'd felt getting off that train. She was hurt and outraged that Michael had kept such a huge secret from her for so long, and that it had prevented them from becoming true intimates. She didn't know what to do. She was too confused. She didn't want to leave Michael just when he needed her the most, but she couldn't see herself as the girlfriend of an exhibitionist. Also, she was just plain angry with him, both for having the problem and for not telling her about it.

Eventually, Rachel decided to stay with Michael while he got back into treatment, but their relationship never stabilized. The pattern of keeping secrets and staying distant was too well established in their relationship and it destroyed the love they had for each other. Several years after they broke up, Rachel heard that Michael had been arrested for exposing himself. She didn't know which feeling was stronger: relief for herself, or the overwhelming sadness she felt for him.

## *Dependency*

If we choose to, in this country we can live fairly independent lives. We can live alone, work from home, and ignore our neighbors. Still, no matter how isolated we choose to be, we are all involved with other people in one way or another. There are people who care about us and people who depend on us. When you're not taking care of yourself because of your sexual obsessions, that affects other people.

Perhaps you don't eat well or don't exercise, you let the housecleaning go, and you don't pay your bills, so sometimes the utilities are shut off. You may become sick because you don't take care of these things. Eventually, other people have to take care of you because you can no longer care for yourself. They then become the victims of your inattention to your own needs. It's not fair to you and it's not fair to them.

# Secrets, Lies, and Trust

Keeping secrets hurts the people around you. Not everyone is good at detecting liars, but most people have a good feel for it. They know when there is dishonesty in a relationship. You hurt the people in your life both with the lies you tell and with the information you don't give them. You create walls between yourself and others that can permanently damage your relationships. When individuals don't have accurate information, they often fill in the blanks with material they imagine. So, some people will blame themselves for ruining their relationships with you. They will suffer because of your need to keep secrets.

There is another aspect of secret keeping that harms the people in your life. Asking others to keep secrets for you turns them into partners in your dirty work. You ask them to carry a burden that you don't have the right to request. You create opportunities for them to feel guilt and shame on your behalf, when they need not feel those emotions; all for your selfish purposes. Asking someone to keep your secret may seem like a small request. But you must begin to realize that it is not a small request. You force the person to be deceptive or lose your friendship. That isn't fair and it harms your relationship. On top of whatever the act was that you want them to keep secret, they then know that you cannot be trusted. Eventually, the person you asked to keep your secret will pull back from you. That will leave both of you a little worse off than you were before you made your request for secrecy.

*Secrets and lies ruin relationships.*

When you make sexual satisfaction your chief priority, you slight the people and the other activities in your life. There's an old saying that goes like this: A slave cannot serve two masters. That can be understood to mean that if you're focusing all of your attention on your sexuality, you cannot be responsible for the other areas of your life because you aren't paying any attention to them.

Think about what you give up to chase after sexual gratification. Spending time with the people close to you, keeping your commitments at work and

*Being responsible and having sexual self-control go hand in hand.*

with friends, and getting involved in your family, neighborhood, or community are just the tip of the iceberg. Maybe you don't get involved with your kids' sports and activities. Maybe you let your partner take care of your responsibilities. Maybe you're distracted at work. When your priorities are unbalanced, other people pay the price. Finally, if your sexual life is way out of control, you are probably mistreating your sexual partners in some obvious way.

You may not show your sex partners any respect. You may never talk to them unless it's about sex. Maybe you hurt them physically before, during, or after sex. Maybe you encourage them to think you are interested in forming a relationship when you are only looking for sex. You deceive your partners into thinking you are interested in them as people. Maybe you force sex on them when they aren't interested. Or maybe you discourage the possibility of intimacy in relationships by turning your sexual attention to someone else shortly after making your "conquest."

*When you are out of control, your sexual partners suffer.*

## Exercise: How Has Your Sexual Behavior Hurt Your Sex Partners?

In the space provided below, list five ways in which your sexual partners have been hurt by your sexual behavior.

1. _____

_____

2. _____

_____

3. _____

_____

4. _____

_____

5. _____

_____

There are thousands of ways in which bystanders are victimized by out-of-control sexual behavior. We've tried to point out some of the major ways in which your behavior affects those around you. Now, it's time for you to be painfully honest with yourself. Who in your life is being hurt by what you're doing? It could be your mother or a stranger, your boss or your neighbor. Naturally, you've avoided thinking about how your actions affect other people. Surely, you've tried to push away feelings of guilt, anger, and sadness associated with causing pain to others. Right now, just take some time to let yourself think about the effects of your behavior on other people and to feel the feelings that come up for you.

Try to put yourself in your sex partners' shoes. Think about what it's like to try to have a relationship with you. Think about the tears and the times they have known you were lying. Think about the distance you created that they didn't want. Think about the love they offered that you didn't return. It's okay to feel whatever you feel about it. Feelings are not going to kill you. Remember not to put them away again, or to make them more than they are. Just allow yourself to feel whatever comes up for you, naturally.

*Consider how you've hurt other people.*

Your job over the coming weeks and months is to stay open to your feelings. Keep feeling the feelings that come up for you when you think about how you create victims with your sexual behavior. Keep putting yourself in your sex partners' place. The reason to do this is not to beat yourself up. The reason to do this is to allow your buried feelings to surface and then allow them to motivate and guide you toward treating people better in the future. By controlling your sexual behavior, you can stop creating victims.

You may find yourself shying away from thinking about those you've hurt. You may feel like getting rid of your feelings or ignoring them. Resist those urges. Once you've opened this particular can of worms, you need to keep it open. Closing your heart again to your negative effects on others can make it even harder to feel compassion later on in life. If you close your heart again, that means you'll keep on doing what you've been doing, living in and creating misery.

## Blaming

Be on your guard for thoughts that lay blame on those you've hurt for what you've done to them. Your mind will try to tell you that people deserve what they get for one reason or another. These people didn't deserve what they got. They are casualties of your sexual behavior.

*Resist blaming other people for what you've done.*

Your next assignment is to set aside ten minutes every day to think about how you've hurt the people around you. Some people think about this when they jump out of bed, others do it while driving to work, shaving, or making dinner. It doesn't really matter when you think about it. What matters is for you to focus your thoughts and feelings on other people for ten minutes a day, and that you do this every day.

### Exercise: Think about the Suffering You've Caused

If you really want to be healed of your out-of-control sexual behavior, this is a crucial step in the treatment. You are going to make a promise to yourself. This is the promise: I will think about the suffering my sexual behavior has caused at [state the time: A.M. or P.M.]. I will think about this every day for _____ minutes each day.

You may find yourself thinking about the suffering you've caused at other times during the day. That wouldn't be unusual. When you finally allow yourself to feel these feelings, they often come up unexpectedly. When they come up, let yourself feel them. Remember that they will not hang around for very long if you don't try to get rid of them. Use your time to motivate yourself to change. Don't get hung up with putting yourself down. That won't get you anywhere. The idea is to see the situation clearly, to see how it really is, in order to change it.

If you have trouble imagining how the people around you have felt because of your behavior, think about what it would be like if someone did the same to you. If that doesn't work, there are many films and books that capture what it feels like to be victimized. Examples include films such as these: *Sleepers, Boys Don't Cry, The Color Purple, Mystic River,* and *What's Love Got to Do with It?* Books about being a victim include these: *I Know Why the Caged Bird Sings,* by Maya Angelou; *Angels Crying: A True Story of Secrecy and Tragedy,* by Tom Moore; *Because I Remember Terror, Father, I Remember You,* by Sue William Silverman; and *Promise You Won't Tell Nobody,* by Kimberly Matthews. Sometimes viewing or reading about a victim's experience enables you to access your own gut feelings about what it's like to be hurt by someone.

If you still have difficulty relating to people you have hurt, write apology letters to them. The purpose of these letters is *not* to send them. You should not expect your victims to forgive and forget. The idea is for you to really think about and feel empathy for what they have gone through because of you. In the letter, you should write down exactly what you did that was harmful, how you think it may have affected them, offer an apology, and explain how you are taking steps to change to change your behavior. After you have written the letter, put it in a safe place so you will be able to reread it when you need to remember what you've done.

## *No Empathy*

One final note: If you have sincerely tried and have not been able to put yourself in the shoes of someone near you in order to understand what it might be like for her or him, or if you become sexually aroused by the suffering of other people, you need more assistance with your sexual self-control problem than this book can offer. Contact the Association for the Treatment of Sexual Abusers (ATSA) in Beaverton, Oregon, at 503-643-1023 or atsa@atsa.com and ask for assistance in finding a treatment provider in your area. This is the largest organization of specialists in the research and treatment of sexual self-control problems in the country. One of ATSA's professionals may be able to help you in preventing a more severe loss of sexual self-control.

*If you don't feel empathy, seek additional help.*

# Part Four

# Mastering Your Domain

# Chapter Thirteen

# Risky Business

An old story called *The Probability Factor,* by Walter Kempley (1975), tells the tale of man who is having an affair. He despises his wife, but doesn't want to divorce her because of the scandal, and he would lose half of their assets. Because he is a life insurance salesman, he is aware of factors in people's lives that make it more likely that they will die due to accidents. These include practices like using certain types of slippery soap in the bathtub, not using a rubber mat, and installing a handle on a wall that is known to loosen over time. He makes sure that his home is equipped with the most dangerous of these features. None of them are illegal. They just make it more probable that an accident will happen. His plan works and his wife dies accidentally in the bathtub. The husband cannot be blamed for her death because it was an accident.

Shortly after her death, the husband dies because of similar probability factors. It's a morbid story that illustrates a relevant point. In all of our lives, there are factors that contribute to bad accidents happening. Like the insurance salesman, if we are aware of those factors, we can remove them from our environments, or if it isn't possible to get rid of them, we can keep them in check.

## High-Risk Factors

High-risk factors are any thoughts, feelings, or situations that threaten your ability to control yourself sexually. You have to know these enemies in order to recognize when they are in danger of influencing your behavior. You must learn to recognize them so that you can produce an effective coping response when they arise. A *coping response* is an action you take to reduce the risk of losing your sexual self-control. A coping response deals effectively with the challenges of a specific situation.

*High-risk factors threaten sexual self-control.*

## Exercise: Important Definitions

In the space provided below, write definitions of the two terms and provide examples of what they mean: Use your own words. Do not copy from the text above. First, think about what the term means, then write a definition using your own language, and then write an example of the term using your own life experiences.

High-risk situations are: _____

_____

_____

An example of a high-risk situation from my own life is: _____

_____

_____

Coping responses are: _____

_____

_____

An example of a coping response from my own life is: _____

_____

_____

In previous chapters we've discussed how thoughts and feelings can lead to the loss of sexual self-control. By now, you know what your usual behavior chains are and how your thoughts and feelings lead you to make mistakes. You have already learned how to combat your thinking errors and how to tolerate the feelings that get you into sexual trouble. In this chapter, the focus is on how to deal with the *situation* aspect of your behavior chain.

High-risk situations are very individualistic. Something that causes problems for one person may be a breeze for someone else. High-risk situations are fairly unpredictable situations. Let's look at some examples before we go into what to do with them. Common high-risk situations include the following:

- Divorce
- Seeing someone attractive
- Using drugs or alcohol
- Family chaos
- Picking up hitchhikers
- Comparing yourself to others
- Being fired
- Travel to poor countries
- Surfing the Internet
- Having access to 900 numbers

- Driving without a destination
- Using pornography
- Parties
- Visiting prostitutes
- Going to bars or strip clubs
- Being alone
- Having an argument
- Having cash on hand
- Having a satellite dish
- Receiving work evaluations

These are just a few examples of the kind of high-risk situations that can lead to loss of sexual self-control. Yours may be quite different from these. The important thing to remember is that high-risk situations are events that move you closer to losing your sexual self-control and they make it more difficult for you to stay in control.

## Lapses

You've already worked on the thinking and feeling parts of your behavior chain. Now we turn to the events and situations that lead to lapses of control. A *lapse* is a slipup or a mistake. It is the small screwup that leads to the big meltdown, the relapse or full loss of sexual self-control. A lapse is a step down the road. If your problem is having one affair after another, a lapse could be asking someone to go home with you, but then not following through. If your problem is rubbing up against people in

*A lapse is a small mistake that can lead to a big one.*

crowded places, a lapse might be squeezing into a crowded subway car instead of waiting for another train. A lapse is proof that you are on the path to violating your plan to change. Lapses are warning signals and should be viewed in that way. They are also reminders of what you are working toward and what you will lose if you continue. Often, they are also part of the chain of troublesome sexual behavior. When you commit a lapse, you may be getting a taste of the forbidden fruit, so to speak.

## Lapses and Relapses

In some ways then, lapses are temptations, and having tasted one, it's tough not to cave in to a total relapse. It's like an ex-smoker taking one drag on a cigarette or an alcoholic taking one sip of beer. Once you've opened that door, it takes muscle to close it again. Know that your mind becomes involved in the lapse too. Some people get caught in a certain kind of mind game in response to a lapse. They start to view themselves as having already failed, as having already lost control. They may see themselves as losers who can't maintain self-control. Sometimes, they use their feelings or thoughts about a lapse as an excuse to relapse completely.

*Lapses are warning signs signaling full loss of sexual self-control may follow.*

Having slipped once, instead of stopping at the slip, they go all the way, saying that since they've already screwed up, they may as well do it right and enjoy it, or something along those lines. But one potato chip does not equal a whole bag of potato chips. Don't let yourself cave in to this kind of reasoning, termed the Abstinence Violation Effect. (See chapter 2 for a discussion of the abstinence violation effect.) It's part of your mind trying to get the best of you and override your ability to control yourself. If you've had a lapse, you need to see it realistically for what it is—a mistake that can be corrected. Remember that you aren't perfect and you aren't expected to be. A lapse does not mean you cannot maintain self-control. It means that it is difficult to control yourself and that you need to work to get back on track. That's all it means.

## Exercise: Lapses and Relapses

In the space provided below, write down your ideas about what makes a lapse different from a relapse. Use your own experiences to describe the differences.

How is a lapse different from a relapse? _____

_____

_____

| Possible Lapses and Relapses | |
| --- | --- |
| Lapse | Relapse |
| Going to a strip club | Having sex with a prostitute |
| Choosing to ride on a crowded bus | Rubbing your penis against someone |
| Giving a hitchhiker a ride | Forcing sex on the rider |
| Using the Internet | Downloading pornography |

Remember, what is a lapse for you might be a relapse for someone else and vice versa. Maybe you can take or leave porn, but the thing that causes real problems in your life is exhibiting yourself. Maybe for you, porn use takes the edge off the feeling that you want to expose yourself. In that case, using porn would not be a lapse for you.

On the other hand, for someone who can't put a porn magazine down and spends all of his time and money on porn, buying any magazine could be a serious lapse that could lead to a total relapse of spending every cent and entire days looking at porn. It's different for everyone. You have to be honest with yourself about what true lapses and relapses are for you.

*Identify your high-risk factors.*

Now, turn back to one of your behavior chains in chapter 7. Pick out all of the links in the chain that are not thoughts or feelings. Those are your high-risk situations.

# Coping Cards

Below, you will see two examples of coping cards, Sample Cards 1 and 2. Later in this chapter, you will find outlines for two coping cards that you will create for yourself. The function of these cards is to provide you with instant access to coping strategies when you find yourself in a high-risk situation. First, read the sample cards to get an idea of how they work. Each card has different material written on its front and back sides, and when you make your own coping cards you will paste or glue both sides of your cards together. Next, read the section "Coping Strategies." Finally, you will make some coping cards to deal with your specific, individual needs.

## High-Risk Factor Coping Card
## Sample Card 1

| High-Risk Situation | Possible Coping Strategies |
|---|---|
| Waiting at isolated bus stops late at night in the hope that someone will come along and wait at the same bus stop so that you can make contact and pick up that person up for sex | 1. Take the train<br>2. Stay in at night<br>3. Wait with someone who knows about your problem<br>4. Don't talk to anyone<br>5. Read to avoid making eye contact<br>6. Remind yourself of the consequences—Take out your decision matrix<br>7. Call a taxi<br>8. Walk around the block and take the next bus |
| (Front) | (Back) |

## High-Risk Factor Coping Card
## Sample Card 2

| High-Risk Situation | Possible Coping Strategies |
|---|---|
| Getting on the Internet | 1. Unplug the computer<br>2. Ask someone who knows about your problem to surf the Net with you<br>3. Watch TV or rent a movie<br>4. Keep the computer in a public place where family members or others can see what you're doing<br>5. Cancel the Internet service contract<br>6. Call a friend to chat<br>7. Leave the house or office |
| (Front) | (Back) |

# Coping Strategies

There are three different types of strategies you can use to cope in high-risk situations. These are avoidance strategies, control strategies, and escape strategies.

## *Avoidance Strategies*

Avoidance strategies are the ways you can keep yourself from getting into high-risk situations in the first place. Avoid the situation altogether. If your high-risk situation is waiting alone at bus stops late at night in the hope of picking someone up, you have to think of ways to avoid doing that. Possibilities include taking another form of transportation, staying in at night, working a different shift, and waiting at the bus stop with someone who knows about your problem. You want to keep the situation from occurring. This is a preventive strategy, and it is the best-case scenario in the case of an impending high-risk situation.

*Cope by avoiding, controlling, or escaping high risks.*

## *Control Strategies*

The second type of coping strategy is called a "control strategy." This is for use after you've already put yourself in a high-risk situation. That is, if you didn't manage to avoid the situation and you need to control yourself. If we use the bus stop example, and waiting for buses late at night contributes to you picking up people to take home, then you can use control strategies to change your behavior. The possibilities depend on how you get the people to go with you. One control strategy is not speaking to anyone who is also waiting for a bus. Another control strategy is to take a book with you and read so that you do not make eye contact with anyone in the area. Using a Walkman and listening to distracting music or the radio is another control strategy. Reminding yourself of the possible consequences is another excellent control strategy. To do this, take your decision matrix card out of your wallet (see chapter 8) and remind yourself of what a relapse will cost you.

## *Escape Strategies*

Lastly, you can come up with escape coping strategies for the situation. How can you escape the situation if it is not possible to avoid or control it? Well, if you are waiting at a bus stop and someone who is a likely target for your sexual advances arrives to wait there too, you can always leave the bus stop. Just leave. Walk around the block. Go back to your home or job. Catch a later bus. That's an escape strategy. Or you could call a taxi, or ask someone to pick you up at the bus stop. When you are generating coping strategies you must come up with *realistic* options. Note that they have to be actions you could really take in the specific situation.

## Make Your Own High-Risk Factor Coping Cards

There are two ways to make these cards: the first is to use the template below, fill in the details, and then photocopy the page. After you have done the photocopying, cut the copied page in half, and paste or glue the front part to the back, so you have one page with two sides.

The other solution is slightly more difficult but preferable because the end result will be sturdier and will last a lot longer. That is to buy index cards, either 3-inch by 5-inch or 5-inch by 7-inch, fill them out with the appropriate headings and details, and then paste or glue the front card to the back card to make one card. Or, you could write on the front and back of one card. Carry your coping cards in your wallet along with a decision matrix at all times. That way, you will never be at a loss for how to cope when you are in a high-risk situation.

Now, you are ready to make coping cards for yourself. First, write the names of your high-risk situations on one side of the cards, one factor for each card you make. Then on the other side of the cards, you write "Coping Strategies" at the top. (Remember that coping strategies are *effective* ways of dealing with your problem.) Then list your coping strategies.

| High-Risk Factor Coping Card | |
|---|---|
| **High-Risk Situation** | **Possible Coping Strategies**<br><br>1.<br><br>2.<br><br>3.<br><br>4.<br><br>5.<br><br>6. |
| (Front) | (Back) |

| High-Risk Factor Coping Card | |
| --- | --- |
| **High-Risk Situation** | **Possible Coping Strategies**<br><br>1.<br><br>2.<br><br>3.<br><br>4.<br><br>5.<br><br>6. |
| (Front) | (Back) |

You may have many high-risk situations, and therefore you may need many (copied or handmade) cards to carry with you at all times. Come up with realistic coping strategies for each type of high-risk situation. Follow our example cards.

The reason for doing this now is that your options have to be handy and easily accessed, waiting for the times you need them. In the heat of the moment, people are not very good at thinking creatively. The pull of sex is incredibly strong. No one does their best thinking when they're horny. That's why you do your thinking now. When these high-risk situations come up, you will be ready. You will have a minimum of three things you can do to break your old behavior chain: avoid the high-risk situation, control the situation, or escape from the situation if you find it cannot be avoided or controlled. There are many ways you can avoid, control, or escape the situation. Be creative. No matter what, you don't want to arrive at the next link because that means you are one step closer to losing control.

*Coping strategies have to be ready and realistic.*

## Physical Signs of High Risk

You must learn to recognize your high-risk situations and then get out of them. It's as simple as that. You know what to do. Now, how do you do it? Let your feelings be your guide. Our bodies are amazing tracking systems. When something is wrong, they tell us about it in one way or another. You'll get a tight knot in your stomach before a big test. Your jaw will clench and tighten up when you are about to have an argument. Your chest will feel congested. You may feel like crying. You may be aroused or have butterflies in your stomach, or both at the same time.

You may be pretty good at recognizing your feelings already. You may know when you feel angry, sad, fearful, happy, or anxious. If so, you're ahead of the game. However, when your feelings are intense, you have to tune in and pay attention to them. That's when you are most at risk of losing sexual self-control. For those of you who find it more difficult to know what you're feeling in the moment, you've got to learn how to tune into your body and how to read the signals it sends you.

*Your body will tell you when to use coping strategies.*

When those aches and pains arise, when you experience headaches, tightness, shallow breathing, and trembling, when your face turns red, your heart rate speeds up, and tension spreads throughout your physical being, your body is trying to send your brain a message. From here on out, the message is to watch out for the risk and to use your coping strategies.

You've been on autopilot for a long time, always ignoring the warning signals that tell you that you are about to dive into hot water. If you expect to control your sexual behavior, you've got to start paying attention to how you're feeling. It's the only way to avoid, control, and escape disaster. You learn how to be good at using your coping skills and controlling your sexual behavior by *practicing*. You have to know your strategies like the back of your hand and practice them every chance you get. They have to become *over*learned so that when you get into a real trouble spot, your autopilot will turn to your coping strategies instead of to doing the same old things. You are creating new, positive habits for yourself. These are habits that will take you toward your goals instead of stealing away the best years of your life.

# Chapter Fourteen

# People Are People

Have you ever been treated as if you don't matter? Have you been overlooked, ignored, walked on, left behind, shot down, patted on the head, or run over? What was it like for you? Naturally, it wasn't pleasant, but, really, what was it like? Can you remember the circumstances and what led to you being treated so badly? Who was there, what was happening, and most importantly, what did it feel like? It wasn't a nice time, was it? We want you to get a real feeling for what that felt like before we turn it around. Okay. Are you ready? Here it is: People with sexual self-control problems often treat other people as if they don't matter, and this causes problems for everyone.

## Objectification

You're probably saying to yourself that you've never treated anyone as badly as you've been treated. Or, perhaps you're remembering all of the times you've left somebody hanging. Either way, there's a good chance that even though you probably didn't intend it, you have treated people poorly. Why are we pointing this out? Once again, the idea is not to make you feel bad or guilty. The point of this chapter is to take a fair look at how you've been treating the people in your life because how you relate to them affects your problem.

Have you ever heard of a concept called "objectification"? *Objectification* takes place when a person is treated as an object or thing, and not as a person. Someone who is objectifying ignores human qualities and responds to another as if that person were not a person but an

*Treating other
people as objects
protects our feelings.*

object. Objectification is refusing to pay attention to the other person's thoughts, feelings, and human needs. Why would we do that? There are a number of different reasons. For one, if we act or think that someone isn't quite human, it doesn't matter much if we don't treat him or her well.

In other words, if we make someone appear to be less than they really are, taking away (in our minds) the feelings and qualities that remind us they are human, we can treat them badly or push them away without feeling too awful about it. It's a poor but widely used way of operating. This is behaving first and considering the consequences later. The thoughts follow the behavior and create more of the same distancing behavior.

## Exercise: Define "Objectification"

In the space provided below, write a definition of the word "objectification." Be sure to use your own language. Don't copy the description given above. After you've written your own definition, then describe a time or an event when you objectified another person.

Objectification is _____

_____

_____

One reason for objectifying others is that people appear to be less threatening if they are not seen as fully human. If people are reduced to mannequins or cardboard cutouts of themselves, they can't bite. They lose their ability to hurt us. In a sense, we make them smaller in our minds so that we appear or feel more powerful. For example, you might view your partner as simply a "bitch." To do this, you ignore information that indicates she is a human being with feelings. When she is sick, you ignore it. When she looks tired, or as if she's been crying, you look the other way. Or you might look the other way when she does something nice for you. You feel better dealing with someone simple, so you reduce your partner to a two-dimensional, lesser version of herself.

Another reason we think of people as less than they are is to keep from having to interact with them socially. This may be the biggest reason why people with sexual self-control problems objectify others. It's a proven fact. People with sexual self-control problems have a tough time socially. By socially, we mean communicating with other people, being comfortable around others, having friendships, and dating and having sexual relationships.

*Objectification
helps to avoid
difficult socializing.*

When you objectify others, you are able to feel more in control of your life, but at the cost of being alone and isolated from people. It's a fairly large trade-off. You choose safety instead of taking the social risks that would make your life richer and more satisfying. But, how can you move past objectification?

## Social Skills

*Social abilities are learned.*

Most people learn how to survive in this world. Some people encounter good teachers and learning opportunities early in their lives. They learn what they need to learn to function socially without having to objectify others. They are the lucky ones. Others are left to fend for themselves when it comes to developing the skills needed to cope with social situations. That doesn't mean that they are out of luck. It just means that they have to work harder later in their lives life to reach the same level of effectiveness in social situations that the lucky ones learn early.

We can all learn to do better in social interactions. Dr. Penix Sbraga sometimes puts off making phone calls to avoid certain conversations. Dr. O'Donohue sometimes retreats behind the stack of books on his desk to avoid social interactions. Often, improving your social skills just requires the opportunity to learn and a determination to practice new skills.

## Communication

Communication can be a tricky business. To communicate effectively people need to be able to listen well and to express themselves. Many people have trouble with listening, expressing themselves, or both. In fact, most people could benefit by brushing up their skills in both listening and expressing themselves.

*True communication requires listening well and expressing yourself effectively.*

When you listen to someone, you are opening up to him or her. The way you listen can send the message that you are interested and committed to understanding. Listening may be more complicated than dominating a conversation, but it pays big dividends. When you listen to them, people want to be around you. They will also listen to you when you have something to say. They will invest in you as you invest in them.

### Exercise: The Basic Components of Communication

Fill in the blanks for the following statement: The two most important parts of effective communication are _____ and _____ .

## *Listening*

You may not listen attentively for different reasons. Sometimes, not listening is an indication that you don't value the person who is talking. Other times, you may be more interested in yourself and what you have to say than you are in hearing what someone else has to say. The problem is this: If you are talking all the time, you have no opportunity to relate to other people or to learn from them. You may become really boring, droning on about the same old things to no one. Not listening takes "relate" out of your relationships. If people don't take turns talking and listening, communication turns into one-sided speech. Then, the person who is being talked to loses interest in staying around.

### Thoughts That Interfere with Listening

Perhaps the biggest interference with listening occurs when you are thinking your own thoughts while the other person is talking to you. You can't pay attention to what that person says because you are busy thinking. Your thoughts could be about what you're going to say when it's your turn to speak. Or they could be about judging what the other person has said before he or she finishes speaking. Or you could be thinking about other matters, especially about yourself. You might try to solve a problem without actually hearing what the details of problem are. You might guess what the talker is going to say and pay attention only to part of what is said, ignoring the parts you don't agree with. You might prepare an argument or change the topic to suit yourself. These are all common ways that your thoughts can interfere with effective listening.

### Exercise: Activities That Interfere with Listening

List three activities that interfere with effective listening.

1. _____

2. _____

3. _____

The problem is that people are born with selective attention. We can't listen and think or listen and talk at the same time. It seems as if we can, but we really switch back and forth. If you are doing one, the other function is turned off. Sometimes, you don't listen because you are preoccupied with yourself: what you need to say, how right you are, what a nice person you can be, and how the other person should really be listening to you. When you are busy with all of these types of thoughts, you are shutting out the other person. People quickly recognize your disinterest in them and just as quickly lose interest in developing a relationship with you. You may leave thinking you were right, but you will walk alone. How can you prevent this from happening?

## *Develop Better Listening Habits*

The first steps for learning how to listen better are as follows:

1. Make sure you get the message.

2. Make sure you understand the message.

The way to be sure of these two things is to repeat back to the speaker what was said. The way you can do that is to use a phrase like this: "So what I hear you saying is . . ." For example, "What I hear you saying is you don't like foreign cars." You can use this type of phrase after the speaker has finished his or her remarks to be sure you understood the message. If you misunderstood, you will be corrected. And whether you understood or not, the person will know that you are really trying to understand. You will be appreciated for your listening skills.

### Exercise: Repeat What Is Said to You

Today, during a conversation with someone, try repeating what that person has said, using a phrase like, "So if I understand you, what you're saying is _____ ." Notice its effect on the speaker (that is, how the person responds to you). Then come back to this chapter and write that person's response here. _____

_____

_____

The next step to becoming a better listener is to show the other person that you care about what is being said. The way you do that is by using your body language.

1. Make eye contact.

2. Lean forward.

3. Nod sometimes to show understanding.

4. Ask questions to better understand what is said.

While you are trying to hear the message, you must resist the urge to interrupt what is being said with your response. While the other person is talking, your job is to keep an open mind and to really hear the message as the person speaks. If you react before he or she is finished, you will miss important information.

The final step in listening well is to show the person you understand what the message was and the meaning behind it. You can probably figure out how the other person is feeling by what was said and how it was said. Show the speaker that you got it by saying so, or with a gesture of understanding, such as nodding your head or leaning closer. When you get into the habit of listening effectively, other people become ready to listen to you and to support you when you want someone to listen to you.

## Express Yourself Better

Expressing yourself is the second half of communicating effectively. Many people with sexual self-control problems often don't express themselves at all, or they give partial messages that other people cannot understand. That may make them seem mysterious. Some people may find the puzzle interesting for a while, but they soon give up trying to have a relationship when the communication never flows.

Lots of things can get in the way of expressing yourself. Most often, it's the fear of being judged, misunderstood, or not cared for that prevents people from expressing themselves. The gratifying thing about listening well in your relationships is that, typically, other people will follow your example and will listen well to you too. They may not know why they are doing it, they just do it. And, if someone refuses to listen well to you over time (given time to respond to your improved listening skills), you can always walk away.

### The Rules of Effective Self-Expression

1. Get the words out; say what you mean

2. Be clear about what you are saying.

3. Be brief and to the point.

4. Make sure your body language matches your message. Don't smile if you are saying something serious.

5. Be straightforward. Lying and keeping secrets are the surest ways to ruin relationships.

6. Talk about those matters that concern you right away, instead of keeping your concerns hidden from others.

7. Do not bring up the past. Resolve issues and move on.

8. State your message in a way that it can be heard.

### Mind Reading

The last point in the list above, "State your message in a way that can be heard" may seem obvious, but many people expect others to read their minds or to instinctively know what is going on with them. But most people aren't that perceptive. You've got to do a little work and tell them what's happening. If you stew over your thoughts and feelings, those thoughts and feelings tend to become intensified. An issue that can be cleared up in a matter of minutes may get blown way out of proportion because you've been thinking about it for hours. Along similar lines, don't save up several matters to discuss at one time, particularly if they are points of disagreement. Deal with them as they come up.

**Important reminder:** If you yell, verbally attack, threaten, or put down the other person, you will not be heard by that person, now or in the future.

If you begin to cultivate your listening and self-expression skills, you'll find yourself living in a different world, one filled with people whom you care about and who care about you. Your sense of isolation will shrink and ultimately disappear because you will have opened yourself up to having others in your life in a meaningful way. Being in relationship with other people isn't easy, but it's preferable to living life in your own "private Idaho."

# Beyond Communication: Basic Social Interactions

Once you are able to listen to and talk with others, your next step is to learn how to be yourself with them. Is it possible to learn to do that? Of course it is.

You may feel anxious around other people. When you are with them, you may feel shy, tongue-tied, or embarrassed. If being around others brings up such uncomfortable feelings for you, you may think that you might as well just forget about it and live life on your own. But living an isolated life is hardly a good solution. In addition to the loneliness, it could lead you to lose your sexual self-control. When you are hungering for human contact, you don't always make the best choices about how and where to get it. That puts you at risk.

Becoming comfortable around other people requires you to make contact even if you don't feel at ease right away. It means moving outside of your comfort zone and risking rejection. At first, it won't be easy but no matter how much it scares you, you have to start somewhere. When you avoid social situations, they only become more threatening.

Think of what it's like when you have a painful toothache and how it is if you avoid visiting your dentist because you're afraid of having the tooth drilled. The longer you wait, the stronger your sense of dread grows, and that makes it harder and harder to go to the dentist. Jumping into the first social situation that presents itself no matter how it goes, and doing that again and again, is the surefire way to become socially skilled.

*Learn and practice the basic essential social skills.*

Doctor Eileen Gambrill (1993), a specialist in social skills, has identified twenty-one skills that raise your ability to be effective in social situations. These can become your social bag of tricks. You won't use all of them in every social situation, but you will want to have them available so they are ready when you need them.

We're going to briefly describe each of these skills and make suggestions about how you can get them to work in your life.

1. **Identify friendly people to approach.** Look for people who look at you; notice smiles, open gestures, and whether they are available for conversation.

2. **Offer friendly reactions.** Smile, laugh, lean forward, touch the other person lightly on the arm or shoulder, keep your arms unfolded, nod your head, offer compliments, and use your listening skills.

3. **Greet people.** Smile and say, "Hello, how are you?" It's that simple. Offer your hand for a handshake.

4. **Initiate conversations.** Talk about a nonthreatening subject such as the weather, the decor, or the music. Avoid asking personal questions right away.

5. **Introduce interesting topics.** Have a few subjects ready to talk about with anyone. These could be observations you've made about current events, movies, books, television shows, sporting events, or celebrities.

6. **Balance listening and talking.** Take turns talking and listening. Listen carefully and ask the speaker questions about what he or she is talking about.

7. **Share information about yourself.** Be willing to tell a little bit about who you are, where you come from, and what your interests are. You can practice this before you are in a social situation. Think of subjects you would feel comfortable with other people knowing and practice talking about them. Talking in front of a mirror may feel silly, but it works.

8. **Offer your opinions.** Be willing to offer your opinion on what's being said. Don't be afraid to be honest. But don't take the position that your opinion is the only correct one. Keep an open mind.

9. **Respond to criticism openly.** If someone criticizes you, listen carefully to what is said and try not to become defensive. Offer your view. If the criticism is valid, admit to it. You will be respected for your integrity and your ability to accept criticism.

10. **Share your feelings.** Let other people know how you are feeling. You don't have to be either an open or a closed book, something in-between often works well. As you share your feelings, other people will share theirs.

11. **Change the topic of conversation.** If you want to change the direction of the conversation, make a transition statement. For example, you might say, "I heard such and such on the radio this morning, and I'd like to know what you think about it."

12. **Disagree.** It's not a tragedy if you disagree with someone. If you are being true to your beliefs, sometimes you will disagree. State your opinion. Allow the other person to state his or her opinion. Offer more information, allow the other person to do the same, and if you continue to disagree, just notice it and move on. You can always say, "It seems like we're going to continue to disagree on this point."

13. **Use humor.** Make jokes and funny observations. Keep the humor tasteful. Leave the fart jokes at home.

14. **End conversations.** Wrap up a conversation with a compliment and a departing comment. You could say something like, "You've given me a lot to think about" or "It's been nice talking with you." If you would like to speak to the person again, your last comment should indicate that. Something like "I hope we have the chance to talk again" would work.

15. **Suggest activities to share.** If you find out during the conversation that you like to do the same activity or that you are involved in an activity that can be done with more than one person, invite that person along. Asking someone to go fishing or shopping is a great way to develop a relationship.

16. **Arrange future meetings.** If you are genuinely interested in knowing the person better, arrange a future meeting. Ask him or her if you could call to go out for coffee sometime, or whether he or she might want to come over and watch the game on Sunday.

17. **Request behavior changes.** If the person is doing something in your presence that you don't like, you can tactfully ask him or her to change their behavior. You can make your request respectfully, and add a comment about why the behavior is bothersome to you. The person may not change, but if you have spoken your mind about it, you won't be bothered on two levels. If the person's behavior continues to bother you enough, you can leave.

18. **Ask favors.** You can ask a favor of someone without feeling any guilt about it. Ask in a straightforward manner. Don't beat around the bush. If the person says no, accept that response without anger and ask someone else. Note that helping other people will make it more likely that they will help you out when you need it.

19. **Respond to put-downs.** If someone puts you down, respond to it directly. You can say, "I don't like what you just said. It wasn't very respectful of me." The person can respond with more put-downs or with an apology. You can either accept the apology or leave the situation.

20. **Refuse unwanted sexual overtures.** If someone flirts with you and you are not interested, you can say, "I think you have the wrong impression about me. I'm

not interested in dating right now." If the sexual pressure is more extreme, escape the situation. End the conversation and leave.

21. **Make appropriate sexual overtures.** The best way for you to make sexual overtures is to be direct. Do not manipulate the other person or deceive him or her in any way. Be honest about your expectations. If you sense resistance in any way, let it go. If he or she remains interested and you have been very clear, go forward and enjoy a safe sexual experience. Keep in mind that mutually pleasing sexual experiences include more than just bodies. Typically, people having good sex talk about their lives and share their feelings as well as their bodies.

## Case Example: John

John worked the second shift at the hospital. After work, he would go to the strip club down the street for a few beers and to wind down with the guys. He spent all of his time and money at the club, and most mornings he dragged himself to work tired and hungover. His ability to talk to women consisted of him saying "Hello" when he put money in a G-string, asking the ladies to go home with him, and saying "Good-bye" when they left his apartment.

During the Christmas holidays, John realized how tired he was of one-night stands, and how lonely he was. He came to therapy seeking help in talking to women. We taught him how to communicate and socialize with anyone. He had a few slip-ups. After learning how to socialize, he sometimes went from the first step in his behavior chain to the twentieth in five seconds because he was so excited or nervous. That happens. But, after several months, John did start up some meaningful relationships with men and women. He became capable of talking with his sisters after years of unpleasant phone calls. He even started dating someone who shared his love of horror movies. It took a little time, but John's life changed dramatically because he took the time to learn and practice these basic social skills.

We've offered you many different suggestions about how to improve your social interactions. You may say to yourself that you can take care of your sexual problems without needing to do this kind of work to improve your social life. You could try, but we doubt that you would succeed. Developing a meaningful social life allows you to let go of your sexual obsessions. It lets you enjoy the parts of life you've been missing, and it makes room in your life for sex to share the stage with love and companionship.

# Chapter Fifteen

# Taking the Problem into Your Own Hands

Masturbation: choking the chicken, whacking off, smacking the pony, jerking off, diddling, greeting Rosy Palm, jacking off, spanking the monkey, and getting off. Whatever you like to call it, everyone does it. Typically, people do it in private and don't talk about it, so nobody is sure whether everybody else is doing it or not. In this country, there's a love/hate relationship with masturbation. People love to do it. Traditional institutions seem to hate it. What gives with this difference of opinion?

One notion passed down through the years held that masturbation somehow sexes up a person. The idea was that masturbation causes the sexual appetite to become stronger and harder to control. Preadolescent boys were the main targets of a campaign to control their masturbation. They were put-down, ridiculed, and shamed for touching themselves sexually. The campaign against masturbation followed preadolescents everywhere. From sex education classes in school, where the practice was called "unhealthy," to church, where it was considered sinful, to home, where it was a source of great shame and embarrassment, self-stimulation was universally condemned.

More recently, masturbation has received less flack. It's become a "Don't ask, don't tell" issue. Only when it is done in public does it garner much attention, as Pee Wee Herman knows too well. The question is, What does masturbation have to do with losing sexual self-control? Does it sex you up and make it harder to maintain control? Or does it actually satisfy so that you are more able to maintain control? Let's examine the issue more closely because it becomes somewhat complicated.

# Masturbation: An Aid to Self-Control

Masturbation means providing physical, sexual stimulation to yourself. When you masturbate, you increase blood flow to your sex organs and heighten your sexual arousal, moving yourself toward orgasm. You can think of masturbation as one tool in your sexual bag of tricks. Sometimes it is done alone. Other times, it's but one activity in a buffet of sexual activities, conducted alone or with a partner.

*Masturbation can be helpful or harmful in changing sexual behavior.*

The function or purpose of masturbation varies from person to person and from one sexual event to another. When we discuss whether masturbation will be helpful or harmful to you as you work toward changing your sexual behavior, it's the function that masturbation serves that is important.

Masturbation is used in the following ways:

1. To increase pleasure during sex with another person.

2. To bring oneself to orgasm alone in order to experience sexual gratification, tension release, or distraction from other experiences.

3. To strengthen sexual fantasy; to create a link between the fantasy and actual experience.

4. To decrease arousal to dangerous fantasies and to increase arousal to safe fantasies.

Masturbation during a mutually consenting sexual experience is a no-lose proposition if both partners are interested. The partner who is masturbating increases his or her arousal, while the arousal of the other partner is increased by watching the masturbation or doing the same. Each partner is touched in the way he or she prefers to be touched, resulting in a satisfying experience for both.

Masturbation performed alone may serve as a substitute for sex when a partner is not available, or it may be only one activity in a full sex life. In this sense, masturbation may meet many needs. It can assist in learning about sexuality and the types of touch that bring pleasure; it can produce sexual satisfaction; it can relieve boredom, stress, or tension; it can be a distraction from feelings; it can be an aid to sleep; and, by leading to orgasm, it can produce a decreased state of arousal in which it is more difficult to become sexually excited.

There's a remarkable scene in the film *There's Something About Mary*, in which an adult male coaches his friend, another adult male, before a date. The coach asks his friend if he masturbates before going out on an important date. His friend gives him a strange look. The coach explains that it's important to masturbate before a date, because that way, you're not thinking about sex the whole night. His friend takes his advice, but runs into a problem. He ejaculates, but, although he aimed at the toilet, he can't find his semen anywhere. When he meets his date at the door, she finds the semen dripping from his ear and thinks it's hair gel. She takes it from him and rubs it into her hair. Her hair stands on end for the rest of the evening.

The coach's idea may sound strange, but his advice may not have been misguided. An idea called "satiation" comes into play. When we are satiated, that means we don't want anymore. We are full of whatever the satiation refers to. We've had our fill of water, peanuts, lasagna, whatever. Satiation works the same way with sex. Immediately after having sex, people are not as interested in having more of it for a while. There's a resting period between sexual encounters during which time interest in sex goes down. That's when people typically roll over and go to sleep. They are satisfied. Masturbation can produce that sense of satiation so that you are less likely to be walking around sexually aroused.

*Masturbating to orgasm may reduce later sexual desire.*

Think about your sexual arousal pattern. That is, when are you are ready for sex? When are you highly aroused, and when is your arousal lower or close to zero? You might think that you are always aroused. Some people do think that at first, but when you really consider it, it's more likely that there are certain times of day, certain situations, and particular people that stimulate your arousal. Some men wake up with erections. That would be a high arousal time. Maybe there's someone at work who turns you on. Seeing that person could increase your arousal. Maybe, like the young man in the film, you get aroused when you're going out with someone attractive.

Satiating yourself through private masturbation before attending events that typically increase your arousal may prevent you from becoming overly aroused (and could save you some embarrassment if you must you address an audience). In other words, masturbation can be a way to control other sexual behavior.

## Exercise: Know When You Are Likely to Become Aroused

Take some time to consider what a typical week in your life is like in terms of sexual arousal. Are you most aroused when you wake up in the morning, in the early afternoon, midafternoon, evening, or just before you go to sleep? Is there a pattern? When you have determined what your pattern is, fill in your answers in the exercise below.

My three most predictable arousal times are:

1. _____

2. _____

3. _____

If your biological clock rings at 4:30 P.M., just before you finish your workday, and your horniness sends you cruising for a prostitute after work, masturbating is a method you can use to prevent yourself from going out cruising. Go to a private bathroom with a lock, and cleanly and quietly take care of business before you leave your workplace. You may think that you would never do that at work; it wouldn't feel right. But think again. Consider what is at stake.

*Do not use masturbation to increase your arousal without letting yourself have an orgasm.*

You could take a break and masturbate, or you could go out and pick up a prostitute, risking your health, reputation, financial situation, job, and family. This is a preventive measure. *Do not* use this strategy to get yourself more aroused without finishing off the deal. That is, be sure you masturbate to orgasm. For you, it would be sexual suicide to begin to masturbate and then stop before reaching orgasm.

Most people masturbate to sexual fantasies, images of memories of sexual experiences they've had, activities they find arousing to think about but have never experienced, sex they would like to try. Masturbating to sexual fantasies is a normal sexual activity. Men and women, young and old, do it. Through repeated instances of masturbating, some sexual fantasies become joined with the experience of masturbation. You masturbate, the particular fantasy starts up, you fantasize, and your hand starts wandering. It's a two-way street.

It's sort of like thinking about a sour candy. Think about a sour candy right now. Imagine how it looks, smells, and tastes. Your mouth might be watering now, when it wasn't a few minutes ago. Memories can become closely associated with physical sensations like eating something sour. Sometimes, all you need to do is think of a sexual fantasy and you are soon physically ready for sex (like the sour candy and mouth watering). But there's a problem with this process when it comes to out-of-control sexual behavior.

*Masturbation and sexual fantasies can be linked together.*

When we fantasize, naturally it's about what sexually excites us. We may or may not want to act out the fantasy in real life. It's like daydreaming about anything. The fantasy is pleasant because there's no work or consequences involved. You may daydream about being the president of the United States. If you actually had to do the work required to become the president and to stay in that position, it might look less appealing.

People with problems of sexual self-control tend to want to act out their fantasies. They may become very involved in their fantasy lives and make elaborate plans about how to make their fantasies happen. Based on this observation, we make a very important distinction. If your masturbatory experiences *are not* joined with fantasies of behaviors you cannot control, masturbation, in the way we've described it, can be a tool you can use to control your sexual behavior.

# Masturbation and Deviant Fantasies

The term "sexual deviance" is often used to describe any sexual behavior that falls outside of what is considered normal sexual activity. The problem with this use of term is that what is considered normal is not standardized; that is, it varies depending on who uses the term. Therefore, we have more precise definitions for deviant sexual fantasy and deviant sexual behavior. *Deviant sexual fantasy* is anything you imagine that, if it were acted out, could harm you or another person. These are fantasies in which you lose sexual self-control. *Deviant sexual behavior* is any sexual behavior that could result in harm to you or another person.

> *Masturbation that is not based on fantasies in which you lose control may help you to control your sexual behavior.*

You can masturbate to nondeviant fantasies to produce the feeling of sexual satiation and in that way you can keep yourself from acting out sexually. However, if your masturbatory experiences include fantasies and plans related to losing your sexual self-control, we have a different suggestion for you. For you, continuing to masturbate and fantasize in the way you have been doing may become dangerous and be counterproductive to trying to exercise self-control over your sexual behavior.

Don't try to squirm out of admitting that your fantasies are deviant plans if they are. Face up to this and move on. We've got some other suggestions for you as well. If you are panicking because we are taking away an activity that is important to you, again we ask you not to worry. We are going to help you replace it with something satisfying and safe.

## Masturbatory Satiation

*Masturbatory satiation* is a way of getting sexual satisfaction and working on your sexual self-control at the same time. This is how you do it: Masturbate to a loss of self-control sexual fantasy, as you have in the past. Masturbate almost to the point of orgasm, but don't allow yourself to orgasm. When you are near orgasm, switch your fantasy to material that is more in line with your goals. That might include imagining yourself having sex in a relationship with someone who cares about you. (Note that if another person is in your fantasy, he or she should be a consenting adult who is not part of the sex industry.)

> *Masturbation linked to sexual fantasies about lost self-control can be dangerous.*

Allow yourself to reach orgasm with the new material that you added to your fantasy. After you have had the orgasm, switch back to the deviant fantasy while you are limp. You should do this several times a week. *You must switch your original fantasy to something appropriate for meeting your goals (nondeviant sexual behavior) when you are close to orgasm, or this technique will not work.* In fact, *it will make your problem worse if you do not follow the instructions.* If you are able to make the switch, you will find that your deviant fantasies become less arousing to you and your safe fantasies will become more arousing.

## Verbal Satiation

If you are opposed to masturbation for moral or other reasons, that's not a problem. You can go through the same procedures without touching your genitals. All you need is a room where you can be alone. For this strategy to work, you say your deviant fantasy out loud (for maximum benefit, speak into a tape recorder) for at least twenty minutes. You talk through the scenario exactly as it comes into your mind, laying out each one of the details about what happens in the fantasy. You have to keep going for the entire twenty minutes. Do this at least three times a week. It's likely that you'll find your deviant fantasies don't hold your interest as they did before you started this exercise and new ones won't pop up as quickly.

*There is a way to masturbate that can increase self-control.*

Research has shown that this strategy works at least as well as actually masturbating (Laws 1995). If you fantasize about sexual encounters in addition to doing this procedure, try to think of sexual activities that would be safe for you, things that wouldn't get you into trouble or cause any harm to another person.

## Covert Sensitization

The final strategy that helps to increase sexual self-control for many people is called *covert sensitization* (Maletzky 1998). It can be very powerful.

1. To practice this approach, you first must get into a relaxed state. Sit in a comfortable place where you can be alone and undisturbed.

2. Take a few deep breaths in through your nose, hold each breath for a long moment, and breathe out through your mouth. Try to become as relaxed as possible without going to sleep.

3. Visualize one of your deviant sexual fantasies, the ones that lead you down a troubled path and into trouble with others or the law. Think about it in detail. *Do not masturbate.*

4. When you get to the most exciting part of your fantasy, visualize something horrible happening. For example, imagine that you score at a bar and an attractive woman agrees to go home with you. You are getting ready to have sex and she starts to take off her clothes. Imagine that as she disrobes you are hot and ready for sex. She strips down to nothing and you are just about to take her in your arms when you notice a horrible smell. It's the worst smell you've ever experienced, and it 's coming from her. It's a combination of trash, sewage, and vomit. You run away from your apartment.

That's just one example. You have to fine-tune the disgusting part to fit your own particular dislikes. You could imagine getting hurt in the act, or people finding out what you're doing. Nasty smells work really well. The important parts of this technique are being relaxed, getting into the fantasy, having something believable and repulsive happen, and escaping *without completing the sexual activity*.

## Exercise: The Steps of Covert Sensitization

Reread the discussion about covert sensitization above. When you have done that and you are sure you understand the process, put the steps of covert sensitization into the correct order from 1 to 4. Write the correct number in front of each step in the proper order.

\_\_\_\_\_ At the most exciting part, visualize something horrible happening.

\_\_\_\_\_ Take a few deep breaths.

\_\_\_\_\_ Get into a relaxed state.

\_\_\_\_\_ Think of a deviant sexual fantasy.

The correct answer to the covert sensitization exercise is 4, 2, 1, 3. If you try these techniques for a month and don't see any decrease in your sexual arousal to deviant fantasies, find a therapist who specializes in treating sexual deviance, or seek information about the medical approaches to sexual arousal control.

*Masturbation, fantasy techniques, and covert sensitization are three ways to control your sexual arousal. If these techniques don't work, seek professional help.*

# Medical Approaches to Sexual Self-Control

Medical approaches generally fall into two categories: chemical and surgical castration.

**Chemical castration** involves taking medication to reduce your sex drive. In research studies, many men taking medication report that they experience fewer sexual fantasies and that their strong desire for sexual satisfaction decreases (Grubin and Mason 1997). A number of different drugs are prescribed for this purpose, including Depo-Provera, Lupron, fluoxetine, and clomipramine. After taking Lupron for several months, a client of Dr. Penix Sbraga reported that at the age of fifty-eight he felt freed from his sex drive for the first time in his life. He had sexually abused more than fifty children. If you are interested in possibly reducing your sex drive medically, you should speak to your physician about the pros and cons of taking these prescription medications. Another approach to sexual control is surgical castration.

**Surgical castration** is the removal of the testes for the purpose of reducing the sex drive. Many men report a significantly greater ability to control themselves sexually through surgical castration. However, both the medications used with the procedure and the surgical procedure itself have side effects that should be discussed at length with a medical doctor.

## The Serenity Prayer

There are some aspects of sexual self-control situations that you cannot immediately control; events like an attractive person coming across your path, or strong sexual feelings that come up unexpectedly. This treatment program follows the serenity prayer model in many ways, although ours is not a religiously oriented approach. In the serenity prayer, people ask a higher power (their personal God) to help them accept the things they cannot change, for the courage to change the things they can change, and for the wisdom to know the difference.

There are some things we cannot control; those we must accept. Some things, however, are within our control, and we need the courage and the wisdom to control them.

# Part Five

# Life Is Beautiful

# Chapter Sixteen

# Real Sex

## Safe and Fulfilling Sex

You may have been asking yourself what your life will be like without having to deal constantly with your problem. Your sexual addiction may have been present for so long that you don't know quite what to do without it. There certainly will be more free time to fill. You'll have more time for everything. One part of life you can't forget about is sex. You might be surprised that we want you to think about having sex. But one vital part of not having an out-of-control sex life is having a satisfying sex life. You might wonder, "What is satisfying sex?" Good, satisfying sex is made up of the following components:

1. Sexual activity that is consensual. To be able to consent, a sexual partner must be an adult with full mental capacities.

2. Sexual activity that is legal.

3. Sexual activity that does not become the center of your life. Sex that is *one part* of your life.

4. Sexual activity that is not secret.

5. Sexual activity that does not get you into financial, relationship, or work difficulties.

6. Sexual activity that is pleasurable for all of the participants.

*Healthy sex does not mean boring sex.*

7. Sex that is not harmful to you or anyone else.

8. Sex that does not involve threats or aggression.

Sexual behavior varies from person to person. Sexual likes and dislikes can differ widely. Within the guidelines of nondeviance, there is a lot of room for individual differences. Nonharmful sex does not mean boring sex. It means safe sex for you and for your sexual partners.

*Positive sexual practices lead to a satisfying sex life.*

There are a number of important principles that lead to a satisfying sex life. Not buying into false ideas about sexuality is a key to having a good sex life. That involves having accurate information about sex that is often easy to miss. Fueling a healthy sexual arousal is another part of creating a satisfying sex life. If you have developed an arousal pattern to unusual, harmful sexual practices, you will need to go back and either take a more commonplace approach to sexual pleasure or learn how to satisfy your preferences in ways that are not harmful to you or to anyone else.

## Common Sexual Myths

Finally, you need to learn positive sexual practices that will result in physical and mental pleasure for you and your sex partners.

### Exercise: True and False Myths about Sex

Circle the answer to each of the following statements as either true or false. Choose true or false for each statement, even if you aren't sure of your answer:

1. Men are always ready for sex.                     T   F

2. Sex has to be risky to be satisfying.             T   F

3. Paying for sex is easier than dating.             T   F

4. Porn doesn't affect my sexual attitudes.          T   F

5. Controlling our sexuality is against nature.      T   F

6. Women secretly want to be dominated.              T   F

7. Nobody would want me because of my past.          T   F

8. I can only enjoy one type of sex.                 T   F

9. Sex is the most important activity in life.       T   F

10. People say no to sex when they mean yes.                           T   F

11. Sex goes bad in long-term relationships.                           T   F

12. Hurt is only physical.                           T   F

13. It's natural to have many sex partners.                           T   F

14. Having phone sex or looking at porn does not affect how I see myself.   T   F

15. The brain is the most vital sex organ.                           T   F

16. A balanced life usually includes sex.                           T   F

17. Anyone can refuse to have sex anytime.                          T   F

Are you ready for the answers? All of the answers are false except for the last three, which are true. How did you do? If you ended up with a number of wrong answers, that's okay. You're learning. Go back and review the statements now that you know the answers. These are the some of the widespread myths or bad ideas about sex. Mistaken ideas about sex affect how we view sexual relationships and how our sexual behavior is expressed. Let's take a look at these myths and see if we can understand why they are so widespread in spite of being so wrong.

*Mistaken ideas about sex ruin sex lives.*

1. The myth that men are always ready for sex is widely accepted as true. The truth is that everyone's interest in sex varies over time, and it's normal to experience periods of high and low interest. Not being ready for sex is not unmanly, it's a normal part of being human.

2. The myth that sex has to be risky to be satisfying is believed by a lot of people who have gotten into risky sexual behaviors and left more mainstream sexual activities behind. Everyone can get into a sexual rut, where the same sexual practices are made use of all of the time. Risky sex can also become routine over time. Two problems come up when you believe that sex has to be risky to be satisfying.

First, looking for risk all of the time can lead to increasingly risky behaviors. That is, you may become bored with the degree of risk that once interested you and escalate to more dangerous practices. Research has shown that people adjust to whatever they have, and they need more and more to make them happy (Campbell 1975). That's why you never hear anyone say, "I have enough money." Raising the risk you take may put you in real danger.

Second, you will always get bored eventually with what you do sexually. The idea is not to increase your risks. You don't have to go to extremes to spice sex up. All you have to do is change your sexual behaviors from time to time, making sure that your partner is interested in making some changes too. You may have given your attention to the association between risk and sex, when all you need to maintain your interest is a change. Try this out and see whether it isn't true.

3. The myth that paying for sex is easier than dating leads to this question: Is it easier in the short term or long term? It may indeed be quite easy to exchange cash for sex on the spot. However, the long-term costs are hidden. Financial problems, disease, loss of reputation, keeping secrets, and stress can be the ordinary results of paying for sex. To achieve a long-term, mutually satisfying relationship, you might have to work on skills such as communication and socializing. You also will have to pay attention to your partner as a human being and not just as a sex object. In the long run, however, it will pay off for you in the form of a real give-and-take relationship with lower costs and much greater benefits.

4. The myth that porn doesn't affect sexual attitudes has been proven wrong time after time (Surgeon General 1986). When you spend a lot of time looking at porn you may learn to look at people differently. You learn to view them as sex toys and objects, instead of as real people with their own thoughts and feelings. According to research (Harris 1994), repeatedly watching pornography causes the viewers to find real-life sexual partners less attractive; to interpret women's casual friendliness as sexual overtures; and to consider sexual aggression less serious than those who do not watch porn consider it to be. Many people also judge themselves for their porn use. They feel like dirty old men inside, because they know when they use porn they aren't the same people with the same attitudes as when they aren't using it.

5. The myth that controlling our sexuality is against nature is a sad mistake. In order to live with other members of society, we must be able to modify our behaviors. Otherwise, our world would become completely chaotic. It's natural to control ourselves in order to live peacefully with others and to live peacefully within ourselves.

6. The myth that women secretly want to be dominated is a very popular one. It flourishes because of the media, where many romance novels and films show women who at first resist being dominated and then give in to domination and enjoy it. The truth is this: No one wants to be made to do anything against his or her will. Often people imagine scenarios that they enjoy fantasizing about, but would not like to happen in their real lives. Think about it, do you like to be controlled? Neither does anyone else.

7. The idea that no one would want you because of your past is an error in thinking that prevents you from having a normal sex life. When you lose your sexual self-control, you can excuse yourself by saying you have to have a deviant sex life because no one wants to have a normal relationship with you. Lose the excuses.

If you give people time to get to know you, they can be very understanding. You probably wouldn't say on your first date with anyone, "By the way, I've had sex with a hundred people." Maybe you would never say that. You can, however, build a relationship over time in which you can reveal the important aspects of your past. People can accept difficult information if it is communicated after some time has been spent in establishing a meaningful relationship. In other words, if someone comes to care about you, she or he is likely to be more open to hearing difficult information about your past.

8. The idea that you can enjoy only one type of sex is very limiting. What happens is that, over time, people develop sexual preferences, sort of like favorite foods. You can eat

spinach, pizza, or steak with pleasure. Some people become fanatics about one type of food, but it can become boring fast. Steak every day is too much steak.

We guarantee that you can learn to become sexually aroused in ways other than your preferred method. You just have to open yourself up to allow new (safe) sexual experiences to take place. If you are fixated on having the steak, you may not notice the opportunity to have delicious pizza. Take the time to look around. You'll be pleasantly surprised at what is available to you.

9. The myth that sex is the most important activity in life is incredibly narrow-minded. We have such a short time to enjoy all this earth has to offer. Enjoying physical pleasure with other people is great, but so are many, many other experiences. Often, people with sexual self-control problems discover that they've missed out on many rewarding life experiences because they were always chasing after sex. Don't let that happen to you.

10. The myth that people say no to sex when they really mean yes is another media creation. When people say or otherwise indicate that they do not want sex, *they don't want sex.* "No" is not a code word for "yes." True, you may be able to turn the "no" into a "yes" with charm, pushiness, threats, or aggression; but that doesn't mean that the person wants to have sex with you. It just means he or she is afraid of you.

11. The myth that sex goes bad in long-term relationships is firmly believed by many people. The truth is, sex can go bad in any relationship, if you let it. Sex, like any other part of life, needs attention and care. If you don't take care of your relationship in the areas that have nothing to do with sex, if you don't give pleasure as well as receive it, if you don't vary your sexual practices, and if you don't make time for sex, then your sexual relationship can wither and die just like anything else you don't take care of.

On the other hand, if you do take care of a sexual relationship and put some thought and work into it, you can have fabulous sex in a long-term relationship at any age.

12. The myth that hurt is only physical is one you know in your heart is not true, but sometimes you might allow yourself to think it is. You might not like to admit it, but your feelings can be hurt just like everyone else's. You might hide your pain so fast that you forget it's there, but you feel it. Your sexual behavior hurts other people physically and psychologically. Don't let yourself ignore the impact of your behavior on other people's feelings.

13. The myth that it's natural to have many sex partners confuses many people. Throughout the media there are so many sexual images and messages broadcast every day that it may seem as if everyone is having tons of sex with everyone else all of the time. The truth is, most people have a fairly low number of sex partners over the course of their lifetime. The average person's average number of sex partners is far fewer than most of our clients think it is. That may surprise you, but it's true. People don't sleep around as much as you have been led to believe. Those who have many sex partners tend to be searching for more than they get out of one-night stands. They just don't know how to get what they really want, which is someone caring, loving, and affectionate. This is a cliché but it's true. People mistake sex for love and are disappointed when they don't feel loved.

14. Another common myth is that having phone sex or looking at porn does not affect how people see themselves. The shame and embarrassment associated with enormous phone-sex bills and porn collections are staggering. In our practice, men with these types of sexual self-control problems relate that they view themselves as weak and dependent on the phone or the photos. Actions that often begin as common rites of passage for many boys become obsessions that men find difficult to put away. Then they blame themselves for not having the willpower to succeed in stopping their behaviors. They demean themselves for trying to quit without achieving success.

15. The statement that "the brain is the most vital sex organ" is not a myth. It is a true fact. People tend to forget how much work our brains do in sexual exchanges. They like to focus on their sex organs, but the truth is, they would never get together if it weren't for their minds. Our brains do the work of imagining someone naked, of figuring out how to talk to that someone, and of coming up with ideas about how to increase our pleasure. That's why this program is a learning treatment and not a physical treatment. Most sexual problems begin and end with the brain.

16. Sex is a part of a balanced life. It is only one part, but it is an important one. Sexual satisfaction, when combined with other aspects of life, can contribute to overall well-being. Having sex that is not risky or stressful contributes to living longer and more pleasantly. You have a lot to gain by making the change to a low-cost, high-yield sex life.

17. People can refuse sex at any time. That is a true statement, not a myth. Some people think that once you've gone past a certain point on a date, or in any kind of sexual encounter, it means that orgasm has to take place. The truth is that people have the choice to change their minds at any time about sex, even in the middle of a sexual encounter. That's because people own their own bodies. They get to decide what happens to them. No one else decides.

Sometimes, a sexual activity seems like a good idea until it's in progress. But if it isn't working out, anyone can call it off. That's one of the beauties of sexuality. Everyone has veto power. That means that if two people are communicating, they both have the same opportunity to make it enjoyable or leave. Men sometimes think that once they are sexually excited, they have to have sex. They may even think that if they don't ejaculate, something physically bad could happen to them. That's an old wives' tale, or perhaps more accurately, an old husbands' tale. The truth is, men can stop having sex at any point without experiencing any negative results. They may want to masturbate later, but even that is not necessary. The brain can wind down the same way it revs up during foreplay. You will not explode. That's a promise.

# Positive Sexual Arousal

Developing a nondeviant sexual arousal pattern is another important factor in creating a healthy sex life. How is this done? We can only offer suggestions that seem to work for some people. There is no surefire way of increasing your sexual excitement for appropriate partners and activities that won't get you into trouble.

Methods to try include the following:

- Masturbating to fantasies of safe activities and partners.

- Decreasing porn use.

- Spending time around potential sex partners.

- Finding partners with common sexual interests who are consenting adults with no sexual control problems of their own.

- Going back to the beginning sexually. Trying out new sexual practices with a consenting adult.

*Becoming safely sexually aroused is important for good sex.*

Creating appropriate masturbation fantasies can help as you try to turn on your sexual arousal behavior to safe activities, and turn it off to the fantasies that get you into trouble. As you develop new sexual fantasies, pick reasonable partners to fantasize about, not models and bodybuilders. Focus on aspects of the person that turn you on. Build on those aspects. When old images come into your head, just notice them and return to your newer, more appropriate material.

Decreasing porn use is essential to having satisfying sexual relationships with real people. Porn actors are just that, actors. They are paid to look good having sex. The rest of us look possessed when we are having sex. You cannot expect life to match or be as good as scenes repeatedly shot from the right angles with hair, makeup, and wardrobe artists to make the scene picture-perfect. If you compare your sex life to photos and videos from the porn world, real life will always seem to fall short.

Remember that appearances aren't everything. Your mind may tell you that your sex life has to look the right way to be satisfying. That's an optical illusion. Real sex is satisfying based on thoughts, feelings, and touch. Those come from contact with another human being, not from retouched photographs.

To develop a sexual arousal for someone, you have to spend a little time with him or her. That means that you need to go to places where you could meet a partner with whom to have safe sex. That leaves out brothels, strip clubs, topless bars, sex chat rooms, and probably bars. Think sporting events, classes, work, social parties, neighborhood gatherings, libraries, shopping centers, parks, and other public places.

Sexual relationships don't have to be for the long term. Sometimes they just don't work out. Long or short term, you are relating to another person. It is important to be able to communicate and feel comfortable with that person, even if only so that you can negotiate sexual issues like when, where, and how.

That goes for finding people with common sexual interests. Typically, you have to build relationships with people over time to find out about their sex lives. Normally, talk about sex unfolds over time. If it becomes the first topic discussed, or if you initiate sex talk right away, you are overstepping the acceptable social boundaries. You are in danger of losing control or of getting involved with someone else who may be in the same danger. Building relationships involves the communication and social skills we discussed in chapter 14. If you are patient and use your skills, you will find people who share some of your sexual interests or are at least curious and would like to find out more about them. You have to plant the seed and wait for it to grow into something wonderful.

Going back to the beginning sexually can be an exciting experience. Remember what it was like the first time you kissed or touched someone? It was the greatest thing in the world. Reliving your early experiences with sexuality may help you to reprogram your sexual arousal pattern.

To do this, find an appropriate consenting partner as we've described. When your relationship progresses toward sex, make a deal with yourself. Promise yourself that you are only going to kiss and touch, nothing further than that, and keep your promise. Practice spending time kissing and touching your partner without moving toward having sex. Allow yourself be amazed by the titillating sensations you've skipped over so many times. Feel your arousal. You don't have to act on that arousal. When it becomes intense, control it (with the skills you've learned), say good night, and look forward to your next meeting. Notice how attracted you are to your partner, how aroused you become when he or she is around. Go a little bit further sexually (only if you both want to) each time you spend time together until, eventually, you have sex together. Don't lose sight of the importance of foreplay. Bring it into your sexual activities regularly.

Trying out new sexual practices with a consenting adult is another way of safely enjoying your sexuality. These meetings can be like experiments. As long as the other person consents to each activity, you can be creative. Think of things you imagine would be exciting to you. Wear sexy clothes, try new sexual positions, read erotic stories to each other, or act out a safe fantasy. Remember, *if the other person says or implies no, the activity is off-limits.*

Build up a repertoire of different activities that are arousing for both of you. Vary them and bring new ideas into the mix. Variety can keep a sex life vibrant and exciting. However, don't forget to keep sex in its place. Being creative is fun and can produce really satisfying sex, but don't let it take over your life. You're working very hard to have a healthy perspective on sex. Be on guard so that you won't lose your new perspective.

## Exercise: Increasing Your Positive Sexual Arousal

Take the time to think about this exercise for a while before you start writing. Then, after giving the matter some thought, list four actions you can take to increase your positive sexual arousal pattern.

1. _____

   _____

2. _____

   _____

3. _____

   _____

4. _____

   _____

# Healthy Sexual Habits

The final part of building a satisfying sex life is to develop positive sexual practices. If you can learn to make the following habits your own, you will certainly start having a better, more satisfying sex life. You will also begin to enjoy the nonsexual aspects of your relationships more deeply.

## Positive Sex Practices

1. Choose consenting partners and safe-sex activities.

2. Choose sexual partners you respect.

3. Respect yourself in sexual encounters. Don't do anything that would cause you to feel guilt or shame.

4. Do what feels comfortable and is not harmful to anyone.

5. Keep money out of all of your sexual exchanges.

6. Allow your feelings to be involved in your sex life. Talk to your partner about your feelings, and encourage your partner to talk to you about his or her feelings.

7. Negotiate safe but fun sexual activities with your partner fairly. Listen to your partner. If your partner says something is hurtful, stop immediately.

8. Take care of your health. Do not get involved in chronically stressful or disease-prone sexual relationships. Use condoms.

9. Be a considerate sexual partner. Please your partner and you will be pleased.

10. Enjoy sex. If you are not enjoying it, communicate about it. If the sex doesn't improve over time, make a change. If the relationship has potential, keep trying to adjust the sex to make it pleasurable for both of you.

# Chapter Seventeen

# Intimacy 101

## Intimacy Defined

The word "intimacy" is tossed around quite a bit, but do we really know what it means? *Intimacy* means having a close, very personal relationship with another person. The state of being intimate is

- Marked by close association or familiarity

- Relates to or is characteristic of one's deepest nature

- Marked by privacy and informality

- Very personal

When you are intimate with someone, you allow the deepest part of yourself to meet and connect with the deepest part of someone else. You may have noticed that you've had some trouble in the intimacy arena. Allowing people get close to you may have been a touchy issue in your life. That would be expected, because people with sexual self-control problems often have this problem, as well. Intimacy is not their strong suit. It is, however, a problem with a solution. That's the kind we like best.

*Intimacy means being very close to another person.*

## The Loss of Self-Control and Intimacy

There is a lot of evidence that demonstrates the loss of sexual self-control is related to deficits in intimacy skills. Three of the most published researchers in the area of sexual self-control, Steve Hudson, William Marshall, and Tony Ward (Marshall and Anderson 1996), have discussed these problems extensively in their work. In plain English, they found that not being able to get close to people goes along with sexual self-control problems.

Commonly, if someone does not having strong intimacy skills because of previous bad experiences with being close (e.g., with parents or other family members), that person may reject the importance of having close relationships and feel lonely and isolated from other people. Loneliness and isolation are common feelings that set the stage for the loss of sexual self-control to occur. It is also easier to lose control with another person, or even to harm someone, if you do not have strong feelings for him or her.

People in intimate relationships report more life satisfaction and happiness and less loneliness than other people. Intimacy occurs in sexual relationships, as well as in close friendships and family relationships, and the ideal situation is to establish intimacy with your sexual partners. That sounds pretty good, doesn't it? Intimacy arises from using the skills for developing close relationships with other people discussed in this chapter, along with many of the other skills discussed elsewhere in this book.

## Regaining Self-Control with Intimacy

It's easier and sometimes it feels better to think that closeness between two people "just happens." This kind of thinking gets us off the hook, and it's romantic. We don't have to worry about building closeness with someone else if it is just a fact of life. It's either there or it's not. However, when we go down that road, we're lying to ourselves. Closeness, or *intimacy doesn't happen by chance.* Its development and growth are not accidents.

Real and lasting closeness between two people develops when both people are determined to build their relationship, learn relationship-building skills, and use those skills with each other. It is a little like a cookbook recipe: Take a pinch of this, add a bit of that, stir, bake, and you'll have something delicious. Keep in mind that we are just breaking down a process that people don't usually notice is happening.

*Intimacy skills can be learned.*

We all practice parts of the process of getting close to other people without thinking about those parts. Some behavior is more or less automatic. The other parts we have to become aware of, learn, and do intentionally. Some people were fortunate enough to learn these skills when they were young. Others have to wait until someone comes along who is willing to teach them these skills. Well, you've waited long enough for a teacher. That time is now. It's been proven that people can learn intimacy skills and that knowing them makes a real difference, especially in the sexual aspect of life (Marshall and Anderson 1996).

# Intimacy Skills

Intimacy skills fall into six general areas we will discuss throughout this chapter:

1. Increasing self-confidence

2. Increasing acceptance of difficult feelings

3. Decreasing dysfunctional beliefs

4. Increasing flexibility

5. Improving communication

6. Increasing pleasurable activities

There's a saying that goes "you really can't be okay with someone else until you are okay with yourself." What exactly does that mean? It means that to be comfortable around other people, you first have to develop some comfort with yourself. Well, where does comfort with yourself come from? It comes from self-confidence, that ability to accept yourself for who you are, with all of your good points and your faults, and to present yourself to the world without apologies. Unfortunately, this sounds easier to do than it actually is.

*Comfort with yourself comes from self-confidence.*

## Increasing Your Self-Confidence

If it were easy to achieve self-confidence, we'd all be overflowing with it. Instead, self-confidence requires a constant effort to see yourself as a valuable, worthwhile person, no matter what. Of course you've done bad things that you wouldn't broadcast to other people. But so has everyone else. That doesn't change the fact that there is a core part of you that is human, lovable, and completely acceptable. However, when you try to think about that part of yourself, your judgments about what you've done may get in your way. That's typical. We all tend to think we've destroyed our good inner core with our bad behavior. The truth, however, is that it is still there.

After the attacks on the World Trade Center and the Pentagon, many people got in touch with their inner core. Ordinary, average guys heroically rescued trapped and injured people. Prison inmates collected money to support the rescue efforts. People freely gave their blood to save strangers. These weren't blameless, perfect people. They were just ordinary people who got in touch with their inner core.

You might try to think about it like this: There is a part of you that is untouchable. It is fundamentally good. It may be buried beneath all of the messy decisions and choices you make every day and those you've made in the past. Try to stretch your perspective a bit and, instead of seeing yourself as a bad or worthless person, learn to view yourself as a worthwhile person who has done bad things. If you can do that, you make room for self-confidence to come into your being and to grow. Your behaviors can be changed. *You can do your life differently*. That's the whole point of this book.

If people can't change, we're wasting valuable paper. But we know from our experience that people can and do make major changes in their lives. What doesn't need to be changed is that whole, wonderful core that you started out with. If you try, we are sure that you can recognize some value within yourself. You can experience yourself as a human being, worthy of life.

Some people find that thinking of themselves as they were when they were children, before they did the things they blame themselves for, can be very helpful. If remembering your childhood works for you, do it. Try to get in touch with the valuable part of yourself again.

Another proven method for increasing self-confidence is to decrease the negative self-statements you make to yourself and to increase the positive self-statements. *Self-statements* are the remarks about ourselves that we say to ourselves when no one else can hear. Typically, our remarks sound something like, "You idiot, you can't do anything right. You screwed up again. Why do you even bother? You are such a looser." A tirade like that can go on and on. It doesn't sound very pleasant on paper, and it's even worse inside your head. You've got your own personal chorus that puts you down all day long. It can get really old and, unfortunately, if you hear something often enough, even if it comes from yourself, you start to believe it.

## Exercise: Write Down Your Put-Downs

To break the bad habit of putting yourself down, you have to start noticing what you say to yourself about yourself. For one week, carry a small pad of paper with you and jot down every negative statement about yourself that comes to your mind. You'll probably see some repetition. We all have our favorite ways to put ourselves down.

Notice what you've been saying to yourself and the tone of the statements. How would you feel if someone else said the same thing to you? You'd probably feel pretty bad. Maybe you'd even be ready to fight over it. But, when it comes from you, you just take it. It's time to stop doing that. You can start the week's work by first doing the following exercise.

Observe your negative self-statements for a week. Write down the most common ones below:

1. _____

2. _____

_____

3. _____

_____

4. _____

_____

5. _____

_____

Now that you've noticed the negative thoughts you produce, you can do something about them. Your job is to notice them in the moment when they first come up. It's like setting an alarm. Little bells should go off when you start in on yourself. After you become aware of having put yourself down, mentally step back from the statements and see them for what they are. They are harmless words that hurt you only if you believe them. Don't put any stock in them. They are just useless phrases—old, practiced reactions that come up automatically—but they are not true in any real sense. They are just words. You give them meaning by choosing to accept them. Stop accepting them. You are better than that. Remember your inner core? Just notice that you are putting yourself down again, and let those statements go. It's like skipping rocks across water. Don't give them the chance to sink in.

## Case Example: Walter

Walter wrote down his negative self-statements for a week. When he came to the next therapy session, he had already made a remarkable change in how he talked to himself, just because he had become aware of the mean and destructive things he had been saying. Over the course of the next ten weeks of therapy, nothing made as big a difference for him as doing this simple writing assignment.

## Increase Your Positive Statements

The other side of not accepting your negative self-statements is to make more positive statements. This goes back to your inner core. You can make statements to yourself that remind you of your value as a person. When you get up in the morning, you can tell yourself that you are a good person and that nothing can take that away from you. You can say that you are a human being just like everyone else. You can tell yourself that *you are worthwhile*. Don't get into listing your good deeds. The point is not to make a list of all of the good things you've done. The point is to remind yourself that *you are valuable* at your core because sometimes we forget that and we act as if we are worthless.

## Exercise: Be Positive

In the space provided below, write one positive statement that you could say to yourself every day. Make a commitment to say this statement out loud at least once a day. It will help if you try to say it at the same time every day. An example of this would be "I have value."

_____

_____

_____

_____

## *Increase Your Acceptance of Your Difficult Feelings*

The next intimacy skill is to increase your acceptance of your feelings. Throughout this book we've stressed how important it is to realize that you cannot keep a lid on your feelings forever. Emotions come up randomly and there is little we can do to control them completely. Furthermore, trying to control feelings actually seems to make them stronger and longer lasting. So, your new approach, and we hope you've been practicing, is to notice the feelings that come up, do nothing about them, and watch them come and go naturally, as they will do.

*Accept your feelings and talk about them.*

Just as loosening your attempts to control your feelings will help you to deal with difficult feelings directly, it will also help you in being close to other people. When you try to be a supercontroller of feelings, you alienate other people. First by shutting down and not allowing others to see that you are feeling anything, and second, by flooding others with your emotions when you can no longer hold them in. This kind of emotional one-two punch drives people away from you.

The solution to this problem is to let go of the strict emotional control you've practiced in the past and gradually start talking to other people about how you are feeling. This doesn't mean that you must display your emotions in inappropriate situations, or that you have to wear your heart on your sleeve all the time. You don't need to announce to the crew at work that you are feeling down. The way to do this is quieter than that.

The point is not to display your emotions but to notice them, allow yourself to feel them, and if someone asks you about how you're doing, be able to discuss how you feel a little bit, depending on how close you are to the person asking. It's being honest about your feelings, not being out with them that matters.

- Notice your feelings.

- Allow yourself to feel them fully.

- Discuss them if you feel comfortable doing that.

As you become more comfortable with noticing your emotions and sharing them with trusted others, you will naturally develop another skill that will bring you closer to others. That skill is called "empathy." *Empathy* is the ability to put yourself in someone else's place and fully imagine what it's like to be him or her. When you empathize, you allow yourself to feel something very much like what the other person is feeling. Sometimes feeling empathy pushes you to reach out to that person with a supportive gesture or word. When you become more comfortable with experiencing your own feelings, you can also stretch out to feel what other people experience. When you can empathize, you strengthen your relationships with others. When people feel understood by someone, they feel closer to him or her, they trust more, and the relationship deepens.

*Empathize: Let yourself feel what others feel.*

## Decrease Your Dysfunctional Beliefs

The third important skill that paves the road to intimacy is learning how to decrease your dysfunctional beliefs. As we have seen, faulty cognitions get in the way of happiness. But that can be changed. This intimacy skill focuses on three different areas:

- Increasing realistic expectations

- Dealing proactively with jealousy

- Decreasing terminal thinking

Let's look at these components one at a time.

### Increase Your Realistic Expectations

People with sexual self-control problems tend to have unrealistic expectations of others. This is a reflection of the black-and-white thinking discussed in chapter 6. They expect people to be either perfect or horrible, and do not allow for anyone to be in-between. As a result, when others make mistakes, as they inevitably do, there is little room for forgiveness and there is little opportunity given for

*Attack your distorted beliefs about relationships.*

others to demonstrate their goodness. This leads the person with sexual self-control problems to be constantly disappointed.

Altering this dysfunctional belief is one important key to increasing intimacy. Notice your tendency to expect either perfection or the worst from others. Remember that most people are a mixture of positives and negatives. Allow them some room to demonstrate both in their relationship with you. Offer forgiveness as you would like to receive it. Make your expectations more realistic and you won't wind up disappointed so often.

## Deal Proactively with Jealousy

Dealing with jealousy is related to having unrealistic expectations. Jealousy tends to come from a set of dysfunctional beliefs about oneself and others. It is the result of cognitive distortions about trust. The underlying mistaken ideas stem from a lack of belief in your own worth, recognition of your untrustworthy behavior, and suspiciousness and reactivity related to your lack of trust in others. We've discussed how it is possible to view yourself as a person of worth in a variety of ways. All of that advice applies here.

Certainly, you have been untrustworthy in the past. Don't allow yourself to think that this means that you are untrustworthy today, or that others are basically untrustworthy. That's the cognitive distortion. You can make the choice today to be trustworthy, and you can judge other people's trustworthiness based on their actions instead of basing it on your early judgments of them. Replace your distorted ideas about how trustworthy people are with alternative thoughts. Give yourself and others a chance to earn trust and, over time, you'll find yourself feeling less jealous.

## Decrease Your Terminal Thinking

Terminal thinking might also be called "dead-end thinking." Indulging in *terminal thinking* is believing that nothing can be done, change is impossible, and you (and others) can never behave any differently than in the past. Of course, this kind of thinking gets you nowhere. This type of thinking is a dead end. If you convince yourself that something is hopeless, you will not be able to see the possibilities for change and you will do nothing to make change happen.

Become aware of your dead-end thoughts. You've practiced coming up with challenges and alternatives to distorted thoughts. Now, apply these skills to dead-end beliefs. Instead of buying into the idea that nothing can be done, consider what you *can* do to change your situation. When you open your mind to the possibilities for change in yourself and others, you break down a wall that stands between you and other people. You create the opportunity for intimacy with another fallible person.

# *Increase Your Flexibility*

Flexibility is another quality that opens the door to intimate closeness. People often get into behavioral ruts. They get used to doing things in certain ways and find it hard to consider new ways of acting, even if new ways might produce better results than their old ways. They are comfortable with what is familiar, even if it doesn't feel quite right. Flexibility is allowing yourself to consider new ways of thinking and behaving. It is opening your mind to new ideas and trying new approaches to life.

In relation to intimacy, flexibility allows for a new, more equal power balance in your relationships; and it also requires being less rigid about sex. In the past, you've maintained fairly tight control over your close relationships to keep from getting hurt and to gain access to sex. Flexibility is about taking some new risks in this area. Risk trusting someone. Risk getting your feelings hurt. Risk breaking up with someone.

*Open yourself to new possibilities.*

When you get into a relationship slowly and thoughtfully, you can get to know the other person gradually and learn to trust him or her, or to back off if the person demonstrates that he or she cannot be trusted. Such relationships can be about more than sex. In them, both you and the other person can get your needs met. In sexual relationships, this flexibility will allow you to enjoy different safe-sex activities, and to give pleasure to the other person that will be returned to you. Sharing the power in relationships and having a greater openness about sex will revolutionize your interactions with other people.

## Improve Your Communication Skills

Perhaps the most important skill for fostering intimacy with others is improved communication. In chapter 14, we discussed the importance of learning to communicate better in order to relate to other people in more positive ways. The reasons for this are to decrease loneliness and isolation, and to create a life that includes more than sex. Improved communication can also deepen your close relationships.

Most sexual relationships need more open discussions about sex. Use your listening and speaking skills to talk about when, where, why, and how you would like to have sex. Negotiate about the frequency and types of sexual activities. Be flexible and sometimes give in to the other person. Compromise with your partner.

Intimate communication between lovers, family members, or friends includes self-disclosures. That means providing information about yourself. You talk about things that are important to you, including your thoughts and feelings, and you listen to similar disclosures from those with whom you have intimate relationships.

This doesn't happen all at once. Disclose information at a slow pace over time. This gradual manner of letting people in gains their support and trust while allowing you to know, support, and trust them too. Lastly, communication about difficult subjects is important in close relationships. If you are being yourself with someone, then conflict is

*To build meaningful intimate relationships, you must listen and talk.*

*Deal with conflicts directly.*

sometimes unavoidable. At some point you will have a difference of opinion or an out-and-out conflict over an issue. Maintaining intimacy depends on sticking with the issue and resolving the problem.

## Conflict Resolution Skills

There are five steps for successful conflict resolution. Don't be intimidated; these are just extensions of your communication skills. These are the five steps:

1.  Identify the problem.

2.  Determine the amount of agreement between you and the other person about what the problem is about and how important it is. For this, you each have to listen and understand the other person's point of view.

To make sure you understand the other person's point of view, do the following: After one person, let's call him John, has described the problem from his point of view, then the other person, say Jane, should repeat what John said *in her own words*. If John agrees that Jane really has understood his point of view, they switch sides, and it's John's turn to listen to Jane and repeat her point of view in his own words.

3.  Come up with solutions that work for both of you. The answer might even be agreeing to disagree. It might be to go to the movies this week and dancing the following week. Find a way in which you will both be winners. Be flexible and creative. Don't just do what you've done in the past.

4.  After you've discussed all the possible solutions to the problem, agree on what you will do to resolve the conflict. Come up with a plan. Remember, you can agree to disagree, and if you understand why each of you sees things differently, then the likelihood is that there will be less negative feelings about the issue.

5.  Carry out your plan and see if it worked. If not, go back to step 1 and keep trying all of the steps until the conflict is resolved.

One of the great benefits of conflict resolution skills is that the simple act of working on the problem together (instead of fighting about it) often makes it better.

## Exercise: Conflict Resolution

Read the five steps above. Then, then using your own words, describe all five steps required to resolve conflicts effectively.

1.  _____

_____

2. _____

_____

3. _____

_____

4. _____

_____

5. _____

_____

## *Increase Pleasurable Activities*

The final strategy for improving intimacy is to increase pleasurable activities. With all the free time you'll have since you won't be chasing after sex, you'll be able to develop new friendships and get involved in more activities with both old and new friends.
First, practice your new social skills. Get to know the people you meet gradually, using the twenty-one basic social skills described in chapter 14.

### Exercise: Improving Intimacy

Name the six steps to follow to improve your intimacy skills. After naming them, try to come up with some examples from your own life. Write a sentence or two about how you will use your new skills to increase your intimacy with others.

*Join others in enjoyable activities.*

1. _____

_____

2. _____

_____

3. _____

_____

4. _____

_____

5. _____

_____

6. _____

_____

## Bring Intimacy into Your Friendships

You may find that you can also use this approach for improving intimacy even with people you've known for some time. Why? Because you probably were so distracted by your pursuit of sex that you never really got to know them previously. Get to know them now. Come up with a list of activities you like to do that have nothing to do with sex. You can go back to your list of goals in chapter 4 for assistance. It may also help to remember what you used to like to do before sex became such a problem. Did you play a sport? Maybe you liked reading, fixing up cars, or walking in the park. Think of things you can do with other people and invite someone along. They will have their own ideas about fun things to do as well. Be open, flexible, and willing to try something new. Remember, this is your chance to create a whole new life for yourself. That life is going to include new activities.

By now you realize that controlling your sexuality is not just about reaching into the sexual compartment of your life, tweaking a few components, and moving on. Sex is intertwined with all of life, meaning that changes in the sexual aspect depend on changes in all of the other parts of life. The development of strong, supportive, intimate relationships is the steel that becomes the framework for a meaningful, balanced life.

# Chapter Eighteen

# Balancing Act

## A Balanced Life

You were told in chapter 2 that this is a relapse prevention program. It is a treatment approach designed to teach you what to do to prevent you from returning to the way you used to think and behave. Why are we focusing on relapse? Because it's easy to slip into old habits. You know that old, comfortable shirt you never want to throw away? Your old sexual habits are like that. They may be very difficult to put away for good. That's why we've created a book that offers you information and skills for dealing with your past.

You were also offered the promise and hope of something new to replace what wasn't working for you. Without such a replacement, you would have a gaping hole in your life and nothing to put in it. Don't make the mistake of changing your sexual behavior only to discover that your life is empty. When you change your sexual behavior, you also get the opportunity to change the rest of your life. You can fill your time with new and joyous activities and relationships instead of the meaningless pursuit of sexual conquests. Changing your sexual behavior gives you the opportunity to create a balanced life for yourself.

A balanced life is one in which there is meaning and room for everything. Studies have shown that meaning, or having a purpose in life, is the major force that keeps people excited about living (Frankl 1992). When there is room in your life for all of the good things life has to offer, there isn't room for any excess. When your life is in balance, there's plenty of space for sex too, but only in balance with everything else. When sex takes over to the exclusion of all other activities, it edges out other important aspects of life, and your whole being suffers as a result of the imbalance.

To help you balance the scales of sexual self-control and a meaningful life, we've put together a list of do's and don'ts to point you in the right direction. Let's review the list of don'ts first; it's shorter.

# Definite Don'ts

1. **Don't forget what your old life cost you.** It may be easy to glamorize your past. If you catch yourself daydreaming about the "good old days," pick up this book and your notebook and review all of your hard work. You can't afford to forget your losses and lost opportunities to do something different with your life. Now, you have the chance to live a whole new life because you are no longer investing in your old life.

2. **Don't stay attached to the things of the past.** Change can be difficult. At first, it will be challenging to talk to new people, to spend your time differently, to avoid certain places, and to say no when you would have said yes in the past. Resist the pull of the familiar. Some battered women are beaten repeatedly because they are afraid to try a new life. Don't be beaten because you refuse to let go of the past. Make room for change.

3. **Don't fail to plan.** In order to live a meaningful life in which you can reach all of your goals, you have to plan for it. Failing to plan results in living a reactive life and jumping when other people say "jump." It isn't satisfying and it leads to the same kinds of behaviors you were into in your past. Think about how you want to spend your time and who you'd like to spend it with. Plan your hours and days accordingly.

4. **Don't climb back on the excess train.** You are probably used to having some very high and some very low experiences. That kind of history has an addictive quality. It hooks you on adventure, intensity, and extreme, although often rare, pleasure, and it allows you to feel sorry for yourself at the low points. It won't be easy to modify your fondness for outrageousness into an enduring, more peaceful way of life. You may have to remind yourself frequently of the lows and the long dry periods that came between the highs. You may have to remind yourself of the costs that paid for your pleasures and pay attention to your newfound genuine enjoyment of life and day-to-day stability.

# Definite Do's

1. **Plan what you will do today, tomorrow, next week, and next year.** Set goals and meet them.

2. **Do a little bit every day** to keep your old habits in check and to build your new destiny.

3. **Challenge your thinking errors constantly.** Be vigilant and on your guard to keep from falling into old habits.

4. **Recognize the links in your behavior chain and take action** to keep yourself from reaching the final link of the chain.

5. **Know the consequences of your behaviors** and always think before you act.

6. **Don't give in to the temptation of immediate gratification.** Wait for the bigger rewards.

7. **Think through all of your decisions carefully.** Don't forget about or ignore long-term costs and consequences.

8. **Be aware of your sexual fantasies.** Don't waste your life planning to act them out.

9. **Tolerate difficult feelings** and continue doing what you need to do, knowing that your feelings will change.

10. **Value yourself.**

11. **Recognize that your loss of sexual self-control harms other people,** as well as yourself. Commit yourself to doing no more harm.

12. **Know your high-risk factors** and how to avoid, control, or escape them.

13. **Learn to be social** with other people and to let them into your life.

14. **Use masturbation and verbal techniques** to control your sexual arousal.

15. **Develop real, satisfying sexual relationships** that don't involve the loss of self-control or harm to anyone.

16. **Develop close relationships with trusted others** to make your life rich and meaningful.

17. **Enjoy new activities** with other people as part of your wonderful, new life.

These lists of do's and don'ts cover the major take-home points of this book and treatment program. If you follow these guidelines, your problem will be on the run and you will be more in control of your life.

## Exercise: The Do's and Don'ts of Sexual Self-Control

Now, without looking back to the text, list as many of the do's and don'ts from memory as you can.

1. _____
2. _____
3. _____
4. _____
5. _____
6. _____
7. _____
8. _____
9. _____
10. _____
11. _____
12. _____
13. _____
14. _____
15. _____
16. _____
17. _____
18. _____
19. _____

20. _____

21. _____

If you were unable to fill in all of the four don'ts and seventeen do's, return to the lists above to see which ones you forgot, and then complete your list.

## Achieving Contentment

Becoming contented with your life is a balancing act. On one side of the seesaw, you must keep your old habits in check. On the other, you have to build a meaningful life full of pleasurable activities. Creating and maintaining the balance isn't easy. It requires all of your attention. You've done the tough work it takes to get into balance. For that, you deserve congratulations. It's fantastic that you've gone all the way through the program. Now that you've come this far, staying in balance calls for one more step: it calls for repetition. Our final job is to help you make a relapse prevention plan for yourself.

*Balance controlling and creating for contentment.*

# Lifetime Maintenance

Problems of sexual self-control never go away entirely. It's as though once you've acquired a taste for losing your sexual self-control, you never quite lose your appetite for it. Temptations will always be present, trying to seduce you into returning to your old habits. *Maintaining sexual self-control is a lifetime job.* You've heard the saying "once an alcoholic, always an alcoholic." And you've probably seen examples of what happens when a recovering alcoholic takes a drink. The results can be devastating. Sometimes, the person loses everything, after having worked so hard to control the problem. How will you cope with the inevitable temptations that will arise? One solution that seems to work for many people with sexual self-control problems is a relapse prevention plan.

*Sexual self-control takes ongoing attention.*

## Planning for Success

A relapse prevention plan is a way to remind yourself of what you've learned, to make it relate to whatever you're currently going through, and to practice your skills every day. There is no cure for problems of sexual self-control. We wish there was. We wish there was a pill that would make all of the risks disappear, but no such miracle drug exists. What we have instead are skills and plans.

By working through this book, applying scientifically supported techniques to your life, you've collected many new skills. You've discovered the keys to changing your life. Now, you have to use them for the rest of your days. Will the work to maintain self-control be the same as it has been for you over the past month? No. In the future, there may be some days when you won't be tempted, or your newly developed, positive habits will kick in and you may not even notice that you are using coping skills to deal with sexual temptations. Other days, however, will present greater challenges.

During those difficult times, you will need the support that you are going to prepare right now. Looking ahead and knowing there will be times when you will have to struggle to maintain control, you are going to create a cheat sheet now that will help you then. Remember when we talked about planning to win? This is the heart and soul of that idea. Leave no room for the possibility of failure to creep in. In other words, plan for the trouble spots that you know are bound to cross your path.

A relapse prevention plan is a short, written review of the work you've done. It reminds you of your goals, high-risk factors, and what to do to maintain control. Now is a perfect time to make your own plan. All of the new information should be fresh in your mind and, at the same time, you've had the opportunity to better understand how the problem operates in your life and to discover what works best for you.

Now, create your own relapse prevention plan. In the first section, list your living, short-term, and long-term goals. You can take them from the lists of goals you made in chapter 4, or now that some time has passed, you may want to make some adjustments to those lists. Be clear about what you are working toward right now.

Always keep in mind what is important to you as you set your goals. When you've finished writing your goals, start the next section and write down your high-risk factors. Remember that these are thoughts, feelings, and situations that put you at risk of losing your sexual self-control; these are the links in your behavior chains.

Be sure to list the major factors that create the most risk for you most often. Next, list the strategies that work best for you in avoiding, controlling, or escaping your listed risk factors. Make a little section for each coping approach: one for avoiding, one for controlling, and one for escaping. Think about what really works for you to not lose your self-control.

Go back to the exercises if you need to recall ways to avoid, control, or escape risky situations.

- Remind yourself how to control your environment, to distract yourself with alternative activities, and how to get support from other people.

- Remind yourself how to tolerate negative thoughts and feelings and remember that they will go away without you having to act on them.

- And, finally, remind yourself to act in line with what you want for your life. You might even write "Just do it" at the bottom of the plan. There's no room for waffling. When temptations arise, you have to use your relapse/prevention plan.

## *Relapse-Prevention Plan*

### Living Goals

**Lifestyle Balance Goals**

1. _____

2. _____

3. _____

**Sexual Control Goals**

1. _____

2. _____

3. _____

### Short-Term Goals (make new goals at the beginning of every week)

1. _____

2. _____

3. _____

### Long-Term Goals—One Year

1. _____

2. _____

3. _____

### Long-Term Goals—Five Years

1. _____

2. _____

3. _____

## High-Risk Factors

1. _____

2. _____

3. _____

4. _____

5. _____

## Coping Strategies

### Ways to avoid

1. _____

2. _____

3. _____

### Ways to control

1. _____

2. _____

3. _____

### Ways to escape

1. _____

2. _____

3. _____

# Don't Think about It, Just Do It!

We have one final point to make about the plan that may be obvious, but it needs to be clearly stated. Your relapse prevention plan will change with you over time, which means you will have to alter it and rewrite it now and then. You will be working with this program for a lifetime of sexual self-control. Nobody stays the same from one year to the next. You will find that you've met your goals and you will need to replace them with new ones.

The people and situations in your life will change. New risks will develop. Old ways of thinking will be replaced by new ones. Your relapse prevention plan has to change along with you. Sometimes you will need to revise it to make it continue working for you. If you update your plan as needed, it will never outlive its usefulness. We suggest that you review your plan at least every three or four months to see if some changes need to be made. In the first year after reading this book, we suggest reviewing your plan monthly because you will be incorporating many changes into your life that will produce more rapid changes in your goals and coping strategies.

You can think of these reviews as insurance. If you're ever in trouble, your relapse prevention plan will be available, useful, and not outdated. Keep your relapse prevention plan handy. Your wallet, purse, or glove compartment may be the place to keep it. If you can't find your plan in the moment when you need to refer to it, then it can't work for you. Think of a safe place where you can always access it easily. You never know when temptation will sneak up on you and you will need the help the plan can provide for you.

# Conclusion

Thank you for choosing this treatment program and doing the difficult work of applying it to your life. If life is better for you and those around you because of something you read in this book, our work has been worthwhile and our goals have been met.

If this book has not been helpful to you and you still have a problem with your sexual self-control, we recommend that you find a psychotherapist who specializes in sexual deviance, sexual addiction, or sex offender treatment for assistance. Sexual self-control problems do not solve themselves. We have witnessed the serious consequences of those that go untreated. Finally, continue the advancements you have made. Do not lose sight of the commitment to do no harm to yourself or others with your sexuality. Sexual self-control is freedom.

# References

Abbey, A. 1987. Misperceptions of friendly behaviors as sexual interest: A survey of naturally occurring incidents. *Psychology of Women Quarterly* 11:173-194.

Abel, G., and J. Rouleau. 1990. The nature and extent of sexual assault. In *Handbook of Sexual Assault: Issues, Theories, and Treatment of the Offender,* edited by W. L. Marshall, D. R. Laws, and H. E. Barbaree. New York: Plenum.

American Psychiatric Association. 2000. *Diagnostic and Statistical Manual of Mental Disorders (DSM-TR).* Washington, D.C.

Angelou, M. 1970. *I Know Why the Caged Bird Sings.* New York: Random House Bantam Books.

Beckett, R., A. Beech, D. Fisher, and A. Fordham. 1994. *Community-Based Treatment for Sex Offenders: An Evaluation of Seven Treatment Programs.* London: Home Office of Her Majesty's Prison Service in Great Britain.

Bender, A. 1998. *Quiet Please: The Girl in the Flammable Skirt.* New York: Doubleday.

Boston Globe. 2000. From an address to the Senate Foreign Relations Subcommittee on February 23, 2000. February 24, page A6. [No byline]

Campbell, D. T. 1975. On the conflict between biological and social evolution and between psychology and moral tradition. *American Psychologist* 30:1103-1126.

Central Intelligence Agency. 2002. *International Trafficking in Women to the United States: A Contemporary Manifestation of Slavery.*

Epstein R. 1997. Skinner as self-manager. *Journal of Applied Behavior Analysis* 30:545-568.

Fishbein, P. 2001. *Adult Video News.* Annual trade publication.

Frankl, V. 1992. Meaning in industrial society. *International Forum for Logotherapy* 15:66-70.

Freund, K. 1990. Courtship disorders. In *Handbook of Sexual Assault: Issues, Theories, and Treatment of the Offender,* edited by W. L. Marshall, D. R. Laws, and H. E. Barbaree. New York: Plenum.

Gambrill, E. 1993. A class format for helping people to increase the quality of their social lives. Paper presented at the 23rd European Congress of Behavior and Cognitive Therapies. London (September 1993).

Grossman, L., B. Martis, and C. Fichtner. 1999. Are sex offenders treatable? A research overview. *Psychiatric Services* 50:349-361.

Grubin, D., and D. Mason 1997. Medical models of sexual deviance. In *Sexual Deviance: Theory, Assessment, and Treatment,* edited by D. R. Laws and W. O'Donohue. New York: Guilford Press.

Hall, G. C. N. 1995. Sexual offender recidivism revisited: A meta-analysis of recent treatment studies. *Journal of Consulting and Clinical Psychology* 63: 802-809.

Harris, R. J. 1994. The impact of sexually explicit media. In *Media Effects: Advances in Theory and Research*, edited by J. Brant and D. Zillman. Hillsdale, NJ: Erlbaum.

Hayes, S. 1999. Personal communication, October 1999.

Hudson, S., W. Marshall, T. Ward, P. Johnston, and R. Jones. 1995. Kia Marama: A cognitive behavioural program for incarcerated child molesters. *Behaviour Change* 12:69-80.

Kempley, W. 1975. *The Probability Factor*. New York: Saturday Review Press.

Laws, D. R. 1989. *Relapse Prevention with Sex Offenders*. New York: Guilford.

————. 1995. Verbal satiation: Notes on procedure, with speculations on its mechanism of effect. *Sexual Abuse: A Journal of Research and Treatment* 7:155-166.

Maletzky, B. 1998. The paraphilias: Research and treatment. In *A Guide to Treatments That Work*, edited by P. Nathan and J. Gorman. New York: Oxford University Press.

Marlatt, G. A. 1985. Relapse prevention: Theoretical rationale and overview of the model. In *Relapse Prevention: A Self-Control Program for the Treatment of Addictive Behaviors*, edited by G. A. Marlatt and J. R. Gordon. New York: Guilford.

Marques, J., C. Nelson, J. Alarcon, and D. Day. 2000. Preventing relapse in sex offenders. What we learned from SOTEP's experimental treatment program. In *Remaking Relapse Prevention with Sex Offenders. A Sourcebook,* edited by D. R. Laws, S. Hudson, and T. Ward. Thousand Oaks, CA: Sage Publications.

Marshall, W., and Y. Anderson. 1996. An evaluation of the benefits of relapse prevention programs with sexual offenders. *Sex Abuse* 8:209-221.

Marshall, W. P. Bryce, S. M. Hudson, T. Ward, and B. Moth. 1996. The enhancement of intimacy and the reduction of loneliness among child molesters. *Journal of Family Violence* 11:219-235.

Marshall, W., and Y. Anderson. 1996. An evaluation of the benefits of relapse prevention programs with sexual offenders. *Sex Abuse* 8:209-221.

Meichenbaum, D. 1977. *Cognitive-Behavior Modification*. New York: Plenum.

Mischel, W., E. B. Ebbeson, and A. R. Zeiss. 1972. Cognitive and attentional mechanisms in delay of gratification. *Journal of Personality and Social Psychology* 21:204-218.

Mischel, W., and H. N. Michel. 1983. Development of children's knowledge of self-control strategies. *Child Development* 54:603-619.

National Training Laboratories. 1996. Adult Learning Theory Pyramid. Bethel, ME: National Training Laboratories.

Penix Sbraga, T., and W. T. O'Donohue. 2004. Working paper.

Pithers, W., J. Marques, C. Gibat, and G. A. Marlatt. 1983. Relapse prevention with sexual aggressives: A self-control model of treatment and the maintenance of change. In *The Sexual Aggressor*, edited by J. G. Greer and I. R. Stuart. New York: Von Nostrand Reinhold.

Ruggiero, G. 1980. *Violence in Early Renaissance Venice*. New Brunswick, NJ: Rutgers University Press.

Ryan, M. 1995. *A Secret Llfe*. New York: Pantheon.

Shepard, P. 2000. White House report made by Harold Koh, Asst. Secy for the State of Democracy, Human Rights, and Labor to the Senate Foreign Relations Subcommittee on Near Eastern and Southern Asian Affairs on February 23, 2000. Reported by Paul Shepard of the Associated Press on Feb. 23, 2000.

Surgeon General. 1986. The Surgeon General's Workshop on Pornography and Public Health. June 22-24. Report prepared by E. P. Mulvey and J. L. Haugaard, released by the Office of the Surgeon General August 4, 1986.

Wegner, D. M., D. J. Schneider, S. R. Carter, and T. L. White. 1987. Paradoxical effects of thought suppression. *Journal of Personality and Social Psychology* 53:5-13.

Wegner, D. M., D. J. Schneider, B. Knutson, and S. R. McMahon. 1991. Polluting the stream of consciousness: The effects of thought suppression on the mind's environment. *Cognitive Therapy and Research* 15:141-151.

Wegner, D. M., and S. Zanakos. 1994. Chronic thought suppression. *Journal of Personality and Social Psychology Special Issue—Psychodynamics and Social Cognition: Perspectives on the Representation and Processing of Emotionally Significant Information* 62:615-640.

Wenzlaff, R. M., D. M. Wegner, and S. B. Klein. 1991. The role of thought suppression in the bonding of thought and mood. *Journal of Personality and Social Psychology* 60:500-508.

# Some Other
# New Harbinger Titles